# ROLF STURM'S
# MAJOR METHOD

For Guitar Theory And Improvisation

Volume 1
Theory & Scales

WATER STREET MUSIC PUBLICATIONS
PO Box 224,
Fairview, NJ 07022

ISBN 978-0-578-02272-7

© Copyright 2002 by Rolf Sturm

All rights reserved. This book, or parts thereof, may not be reproduced in any manner without written permission from the publisher.

# ACKNOWLEDGEMENTS

Thanks to John Abercrombie for his kind words and contributions to jazz guitar.

Thanks to Howard Alden for his kind words and contributions to jazz guitar.

Thanks to Rick Dandes for his kind words and support.

Thanks to Jody Espina for his kind words and encouragement towards this book.

Thanks to John Stroud for the fantastic cover design.

Thanks to Greg Heisler for the back cover photo.

Thanks to Rob Henke, Jody Espina, Leese Walker, Frank Fagnano, Tomas Ulrich, Tony Trischka, Walter Thompson, Joe Gallant, Pablo Aslan, Raul Jalrena, Brian Babcock, Grisha Alexiev, Kermit Driscoll.... and others, just too numerous to mention here (you know who you are!) for sharing your time and talents in helping to make such wonderful music.

Thanks to Joe Pass, Jim Hall, John Abercrombie, Bill Frisell, Dana Wilson, Steve Brown, and Harry Leahey for sharing your musical knowledge with me.

Thanks to Margie & Douglas Sturm, Leese Walker, Hans, Jackie & Wolfgang Sturm, for their unending support, love and caring.

# NOTES

The "Major Method" is a revolutionary approach to music theory for guitarists. You will learn all of the scales that are needed to solo through even the most advanced tunes, in an amazingly short period of time. First, you learn the major scale on the guitar. Then, almost all of the other scales will be related back to the major scale (usually with only one note difference). This drastically reduces the amount of time and effort that it takes to learn these other scales.

Music theory is almost always explained through the piano or keyboard because it is all laid out in front of you from left to right and it can be easily understood this way. The information contained in this book deals with the *"yeah, but how does that apply to the guitar?"* questions.

I have also included some explanations of a few of the larger theoretical concepts and history. This information might seem extraneous, but it can open your eyes and ears to a much greater understanding of how and why things work together.

Throughout this book I have used diagrams that are drawn in a similar way to how tabliture is constructed. This means that the headstock of the guitar is on the left and the body of the guitar is on the right. This is as if you are looking down at your guitar while you are playing. I've done this because, while you'll never encounter tabliture in a professional playing situation (it is used almost exclusively for educational or transcription purposes), it is widely used in the guitar education community, and it might be confusing to many of our guitar brethren if I drew the diagrams any other way.

A HUGE area that this book does NOT cover is reading music. Guitar players are notoriously bad readers. This is a problem. If you're going to be a musician, then you need to be able to read and write music. Luckily, there are numerous resources out there available for us to learn how to read... check them out. And YES, there are examples of noted guitarists who can't read music, this is NOT something to celebrate or emulate.

ENJOY THE BOOK!!

# TABLE OF CONTENTS

| | |
|---|---|
| "Major Method" | i |
| In The Beginning | 1 |
| Chromatic Scale | 3 |
| Major Scale (Pure/Natural Minor) | 4 |
| Major Scale Patterns | 10 |
| What's Next? | 16 |
| Now What? | 17 |
| Pentatonic Scale | 21 |
| Pentatonic Scale Patterns | 23 |
| Name Game (Blues Scale) | 28 |
| What About Chords? (Chord Intro) | 34 |
| Three Note Chords (Barre Chords) | 35 |
| Barre Chord Diagrams | 37 |
| Four Note Chords (Seventh Chords) | 53 |
| Seventh Chord Diagrams | 55 |
| Harmonic Minor | 75 |
| Melodic Minor | 82 |
| Whole Tone | 90 |
| Diminished | 96 |
| Cycle Of What?!? (5ths) | 102 |
| Blues | 111 |
| What To Do | 114 |

# MAJOR METHOD

The Major Method is an approach that I came up with for learning music theory on the neck of the guitar. The neck of the guitar has a lot of different patterns and shapes to learn in order to know one simple major scale. Then you have to tie all of these patterns together so they appear as one huge pattern on the entire neck.

To approach "major", "pure/natural minor", "major pentatonic", "minor pentatonic", "blues", "harmonic minor", and "melodic minor" all as completely different and distinct intervalic structures (each requiring a whole new set of patterns), makes for an enormous pile of work!

It doesn't have to be so difficult... PARTICULARLY WHEN ALL OF THESE SCALES SHARE SO MANY OF THE SAME BASIC SHAPES!!

The Major Method relates ALL of these scales back to the shapes and patterns of the major scale (hence the name "Major Method"... catchy, eh?).

While the theory of this system will work for any instrument, it is particularly designed for the guitar. Music theory on the guitar is extremely visual (at least in the beginning). "Seeing" all of the notes of one major scale on the entire neck of the guitar is a fairly large task (much more involved than learning a major scale on most other instruments).

Most of these other scales that one needs to know in order to become an accomplished improviser use EXACTLY the same shapes as the major scale, with the exception (usually) of just one note per octave.

For other instruments, this might seem like a distraction from the way that they think of these other scales, but for the guitar, it provides you with all of the possible notes for soloing and chord construction on the entire neck with the LEAST amount of effort...
...beyond learning the major scale patterns.

There are many ways to organize the information that you'll need in order to become an improvising guitarist. The "Major Method" Volume 1 presents the scale patterns that you'll need to know and some of the basic chord shapes that you'll need to know.

Chords basically come from scales, so Volume 1 primarily deals with the essential scales and the theory behind them.

The material covered in Volume 1 includes:

I <u>SCALES</u>:
    1) Major scale (major scale & pure/natural minor scale)
    2) Pentatonic scale (major pentatonic & minor pentatonic)
    3) Blues scale
    4) Harmonic minor scale
    5) Melodic minor scale
    6) Whole tone scale
    7) Diminished scale

II <u>CHORDS</u>:
    1) Barre chords (three note chords)
    2) Seventh chords (four note chords)...... an introduction.

This will provide you with a LARGE chunk of raw information that will get you started on your guitar improv quest. There is, of course, more information that you will need to know.

You will also need to learn:
- How to use all of this information: "When and how can I use all of these different scales?!?" etc...

- There are many other types of chords (inversions, extensions, alterations, etc.) that need to be learned.

- And of course the great missing link between the scales and the chords.... arpeggios.

More of this information will be provided in easily digestible clumps in Volume 2... (appetizing eh?).

Before diving head-long into the scale patterns, I will provide you with my 25 cent explanation of music and where its coming from. I'll also provide some background information about music theory, the chromatic scale, and the major scale. You may be tempted to skip this stuff... but this is the stuff that will answer an awful lot of those questions that you have right now AND those questions that ARE going to crop up...
...(check it out).

# IN THE BEGINNING...
(the 25 cent explanation of music)

**Music is organized sound.**
You could sample or record a few everyday sounds (coughing, flushing the toilet, banging your toe on the coffee table.... again!!), put them in an order that pleases you, and play them back. This would be your very own "symphony of daily life".

**Sound (in our environment... on earth) is vibration.**
If you could wave or vibrate your arm fast enough, you would be able to hear a sound, much like the whistling of the wind (or the screaming of pain that you'd be in from moving your arm that fast).

The faster something vibrates, the higher in pitch it becomes. The slower something vibrates, the lower in pitch it becomes. We have a somewhat limited range in our hearing capability. Sound travels both higher and lower than what we can hear. It kind of makes one wonder what sorts of symphonies or secret communications are happening in those frequencies that we can't hear. Dogs can hear sounds that are higher than what we can hear. When we blow a dog whistle, we can't hear anything, but dogs go nuts. When whales migrate, they sing songs that can go both higher and lower than what we can hear. What are those dangerous creatures up to?...

(just because you're paranoid, doesn't mean they're not out to get you).

So, within our limited hearing spectrum, we've divided the range of vibration into chunks of sound that we call octaves. If something vibrates 440 times a second, we call it: "A 440". Most folks in the United States tune their instruments to A 440, but this vibration is not universal. Some orchestras in Europe tune to A 442 or even A 443, making everything just a little bit higher in pitch.

If you were to double this A 440 vibration to 880, you would come to the next higher octave. This frequency would be "A 880". We can hear a bunch of different octaves. Pianos generally have just over a 7 octave range and we can hear notes above and below the piano's range. Of course, everyone's hearing capabilities are a little different. We tend to loose some of our high frequency hearing as we get older (or if we've played a lot of really loud rehearsals, gigs, or jam sessions!!).

Within this octave chunk, we've divided the range of vibration into 12 different pitches. The distance between each of these pitches (the increased or decreased number of vibrations it takes to get to the next pitch), we call half steps.

Other cultures may have more or less divisions within this octave, like the quarter steps (tones) used in Balinese gamelon music or the half sharps and half flats used in Middle Eastern music. So these other systems may have more or less notes per octave then this particular system that we're using.

These 12 different pitches that make up an octave, we call the **"CHROMATIC"** scale... (a fancy name for all of the notes that are possible... in this system). There are types of music that uses all 12 pitches. One such type of music is called 12 tone music.

*12 tone music (also called "serial" music) is considered a contemporary classical form of composition where you put all 12 pitches into whatever order you like (this is called your "tone row"). Then you compose using the tones in this order, or you can also make a graph of the notes and use them going forwards, backwards, in retrograde, or inverted etc... While this music is harmonically quite egalitarian and very mathematically stable, to many the end result sounds pretty random and a bit bizarre. Perhaps we're just not used to this yet and this is the direction that we're headed in music... perhaps.

HOWEVER, this 12 tone music is still a bit too weird for most, so a more consonant or stable sounding system for composition and organizing these pitches is more popular... (the MAJOR scale).

* This definition of 12 tone music is a thumbnail sketch of the real deal. My apologies to the 12 tone society for any misrepresentation through simplification that I have made of your name-sake.

# CHROMATIC SCALE
## (The mother of all scales)

In the chromatic scale, every note is one half step apart from each other. This scale represents all of the notes that are possible within this system of music. One octave of the <u>CHROMATIC SCALE</u> looks like this:

E   F   (F#/Gb)   G   (G#/Ab)   A   (A#/Bb)   B   C   (C#/Db)   D   (D#/Eb)   E

"Up" in pitch is from left to right. The two notes in each set of parenthesis are the same pitch with two different names. These notes are called "enharmonic". So F# is the enharmonic equivalent of Gb... and visa-versa.

> \# is a sharp.
> > It raises a pitch by a half step (on the guitar this is one fret).
>
> b is a flat.
> > It lowers the pitch by a half step (on the guitar this is one fret).
>
> ♮ is a natural.
> > It cancels out any sharp or flat.
> > (these symbols are also seen when reading music)

So, again, as seen above, an F# (a raised F) is the same note as a Gb (a lowered G).

I started this diagram with letter E, because the lowest string on the guitar is an E. Each letter name that follows to the right represents the next fret up on the neck of the guitar. Notice that there are no half steps between E-F and B-C.

Notice that there are 12 different pitches in the octave before you reach another E... (12 notes to an octave... double dots on the 12th fret of the guitar... hmmm).

Once you get up to the octave (12 frets), all the letter names begin again and repeat themselves in the next octave. So E is followed by F, F is followed by F#, etc. On the guitar, the note on the 12th fret of each string has the same letter name as the open string name. The letter name of the note on the 1st fret is the same as that on the 13th fret, the 2nd fret's name is the same as the 14th fret's name and so on.

# THE MAJOR SCALE

The major scale is one of the most common grouping of notes that is used when improvising. It has 7 different notes per octave. These 7 different notes come from the chromatic scale. The chromatic scale is that strange name given to all the notes that are possible within this particular system of music (...that we just went over).

Before diving into the major scale, there are some concepts that need to be introduced to make this all a little more understandable...

Note: references to up or down are usually in relation to pitch. So, up the neck means towards the body of the guitar. Down the neck means towards the head stock of the guitar. Also, the strings of the guitar are set up so that the "high" E string is the lowest string in relation to gravity. However, it is called the first string and it is the highest string. And, you guessed it, the "low" E string is the thick string that is on the top, gravitationally speaking, but it's called the sixth string and it is the lowest string.

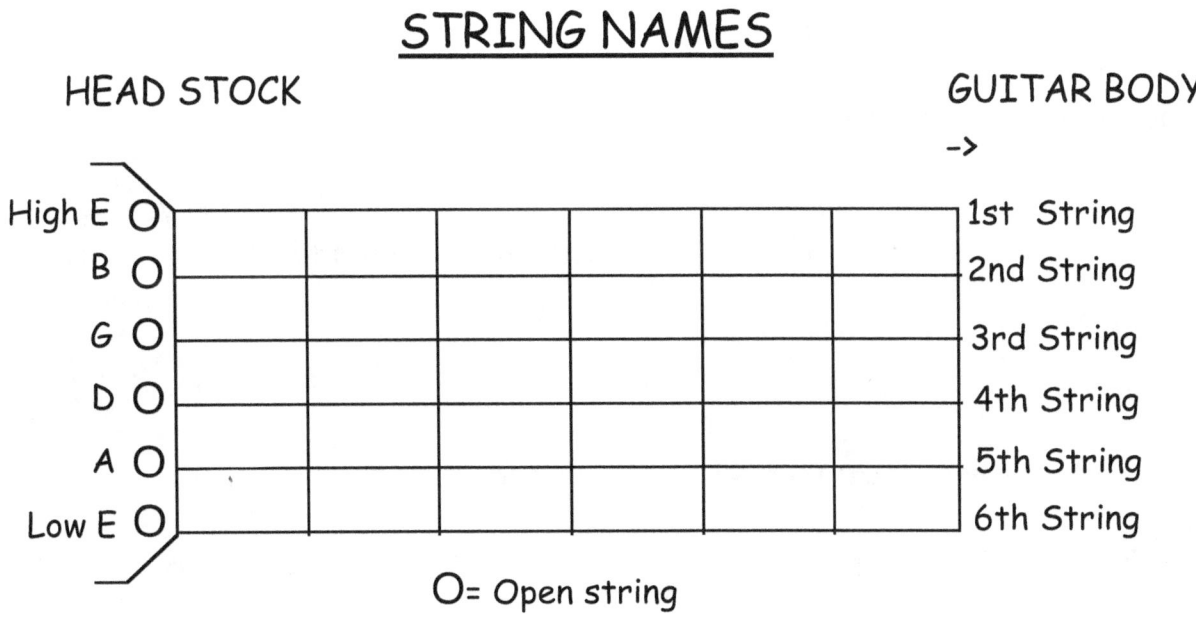

Eventually you will have to know the letter names of the notes all over the neck. But you will definitely need to know the letter names of the notes on the low E string immediately. So here they are:

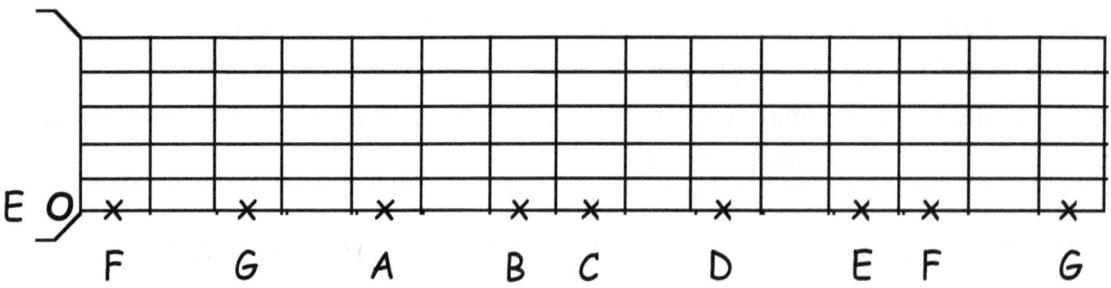

The open (O) E string is... an E (brilliant, right?). The X's are where the corresponding letter names live. The frets in between the X's on this diagram are where the #'s and b's live.

Remember:

# = sharp and this raises the pitch (one fret to the right of a letter)
b = flat and this lowers the pitch (one fret to the left of a letter)


So the fret between F and G is called an F# or a Gb.
The fret between G and A is called a G# or an Ab etc...
(this should all sound a bit familiar).

Knowing these letter names will be vital to being able to play in different keys. It's not as difficult as it looks and there are plenty of short cuts to help you memorize this.

For instance:

All of the letter names repeat themselves once you get up to the 12th fret.

The 5th fret is an A, which matches the letter name of the next open string.

All letters are two frets apart except E to F and B to C.

Once again, the MAJOR SCALE is a group of 7 notes that comes from the chromatic scale (this is the "do, re, mi, fa, sol, la, ti, do" business that you've heard so much about). Using only 7 notes means that some of the 12 notes from the chromatic scale have to be left out or skipped over. In order to figure out which notes to leave out, a major scale pattern of whole steps and half steps was designed.

The pattern is: W W H W W W H

W = whole step (which, for us, means two frets: you skip a note)
H = half step (which, for us, means one fret: you don't skip a note)

Here is a chromatic scale that goes 3 half steps more than one octave. I've done this for a reason that'll become clear in a minute or two.

E  F  [F#/Gb]  G  [G#/Ab]  A  [A#/Bb]  B  C  [C#/Db]  D  [D#/Eb]  E  F  [F#/Gb]  G

You can start a major scale on any one of the notes from the chromatic scale. Whichever note you start on, is the name of that major scale. So if you start on the letter C, you are in the C major scale. This first pitch is also referred to as the key. So you would also be in the key of C major. Since there are 12 different pitches in the chromatic scale, there are 12 possible major scales or keys. Keep in mind that all of these scales or keys have the same intervalic structure (the same whole step and half step patterns).

Now you need to know how to get the rest of the notes for a complete major scale. Since G major seems to be a guitar-friendly key, I'll show you how to figure out the rest of the notes for the G major scale. If you're in the key of G, the first note is a G. To get to the second note, you have to go "up" (from left to right) one whole step in the chromatic scale. This would mean skipping the note that has both the G# and Ab names and arriving at the A. Now A is the second note and to get to the third, you have to go "up" another whole step. Skipping over the A#/Bb, you arrive at B. So far things look like this:

```
                    W   W   H   W   W   W   H
                    /\  /\  /\  /\  /\  /\  /\
    MAJOR SCALE:    1   2   3   4   5   6   7   1
       ( key of )  [G]  A   B
```

(Note: all notes are a whole step apart except the 3 to 4 and the 7 to 1)

Once you've figured out what all of the notes are for the G major scale, things should look like this:

(Those 3 extra half steps on the chromatic scale diagram should have helped)

You can find a G on the third fret of the low E string and play this major scale up the neck, staying entirely on the low E string. This is the G major scale.
And it looks something like this:

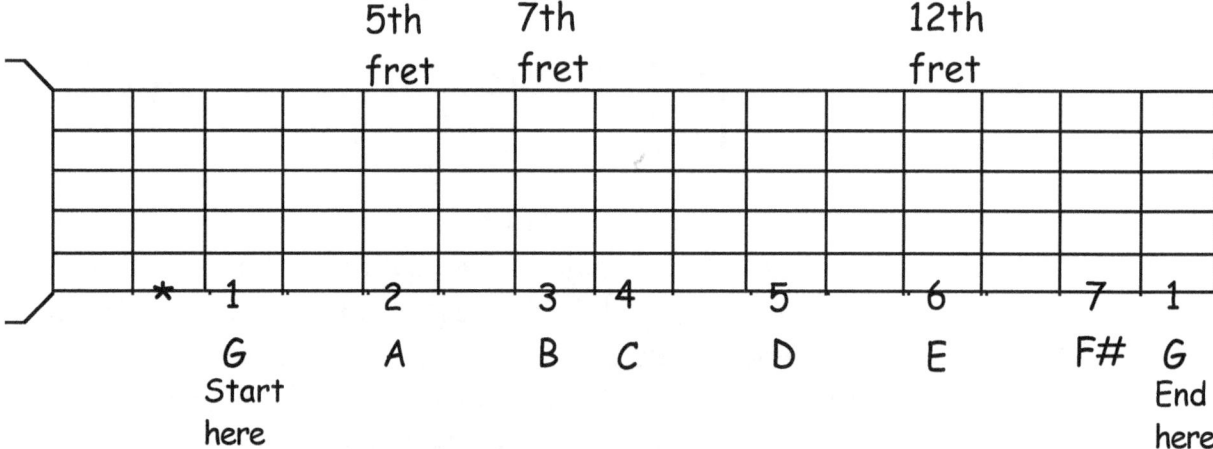

Playing the G major scale like this means moving your left hand quite a bit. This much movement makes it difficult to play the scale quickly and you've only learned one string. So what we're going to do is learn the scale across the strings in shapes that can be played within one hand position. This means learning 7 different patterns, each one starting with a different scale degree.

The lowest pattern of the G major scale that can be played on the neck of the guitar, without using open strings, is pattern 7. We're not talkin' about the 7 on the 14th fret, but the 7 that's on the 2nd fret. *Remember, there is always a 7 just one fret below (to the left of) the 1. This is a good place to start for a couple of reasons:

    1) It's the lowest pattern in the key of G major (closest to the headstock).
    2) It's one of the patterns that doesn't have any finger stretches!!

Even though we're learning pattern 7 first, REMEMBER that the 1 is the name of the major scale NOT the 7.

And another thing....

# Two Names...One Scale!
## G "Major"/E "Pure Minor"

Every major scale has 7 different scale degrees (notes). Every major scale's name comes from its "starting" pitch (from the 1). **Every major scale also has a relative minor name.** So the 7 major scale patterns that you're about to learn have two names; a major name and a minor name. The minor name comes from the scale's 6th pitch. In the G major scale, "E" is the 6th pitch. "E" is the relative minor of G major. So these 7 patterns that you're about to learn, have two names: the G major scale and the E minor scale. Technically this is the E "pure minor" or the E "natural minor" scale. Many times the words "pure" or "natural" are dropped when referring to this scale and it is just called the minor scale. These words are used to distinguish it from the other minor scales. There are two other types of minor scales that are commonly used when improvising: the melodic minor and the harmonic minor. These scales are always referred to as "melodic" minor or "harmonic" minor.

Music theory folk like to think of the "pure/natural" minor scale as a separate entity from the major scale and will assign a whole new set of numbers to the scale degrees. Their reasoning is that since the 6th is the new "starting" pitch, it should now be considered the new 1, the 7 becomes the new 2, the 1 becomes the new b3, etc...

**However:**
1) When improvising, you don't have to "start" on the first pitch of any scale, so its not important to call the theoretical first pitch of the scale a "1". What is important is that you know where all of the available notes are and that you can begin to use them to try and make music.

2) All of the shapes on the neck of the guitar **are excactly the same** for the major scale as they are for the minor scale. And you already have the pitches numbered as a point of reference, so why not just use the numbers that are already there?!? Besides, the new numbers that the music theory folk give to the pure/natural minor scale degrees are all based on how the intervals relate to the major scale intervals anyway!

Also, by always using one set of pitch numbers, you create less confusion when learning the shapes of other scales (particularly when the other scales share so many of the same or similar shapes).

# "MAJOR METHOD VS TRADITIONAL"
## (NATURAL OR PURE MINOR)

TRADITIONALLY, the natural minor scale is taught as being a major scale with a b3, b6, & b7. For guitarists, this means re-learning all 7 major scale patterns with 3 changed notes per octave!

```
               1   2   3   4   5   6   7   1
    E major:   E   F#  G#  A   B   C#  D#  E

               1   2   b3  4   5   b6  b7  1
E natural minor: E  F#  G   A   B   C   D   E
```

The MAJOR METHOD teaches the natural minor scale as just being based on the 6th scale degree of the relative major scale. So E natural minor is the same as the G major scale, starting on the 6th scale degree, and you have no new patterns or numbers to learn:

```
               1  2  3  4  5  6  7  1
    G major:   G  A  B  C  D  E  F# G
                           6  7  1  2  3  4  5  6
E natural minor:           E  F# G  A  B  C  D  E
```

The numbers stay the same AND all 7 patterns stay the same! In the past, this visual approach to learning the neck of the guitar (learning the shapes of the scales on the neck) has been criticized as a short-cut. It was thought that one should learn the sound of the scale through reading music and eventually come to realize all of the shapes of a scale through years of reading and study. This may have some validity, and it would certainly make guitar players better music readers. But it would also make us all fifty or sixty years old before we'd know the entire neck of the guitar and most of us are just too damn impatient! So, we just have to be vigilant in our pursuit of "HEARING THE SHAPES" and trust that eventually we will begin to "see" (in our mind's eye) what we want to play and what we are hearing in our heads and hearts.

**NOTES ON PLAYING:** For now, when you play these patterns just use a down stroke with your guitar pick for each note. Make sure that you only pick the string that you need (this is not as easy as it sounds). Also, make sure that your right hand is picking the same string that your left hand is fingering... (this sounds obvious, but, again, it's not as easy as it sounds). Run all of these patterns forwards AND backwards.

ALRIGHT!! NOW....AT LONG LAST, HERE ARE THE MAJOR SCALE PATTERNS:

# G "Major" & E "Pure Minor" Scale Shapes

The small numbers represent the Major scale pitches:
1=G  2=A  3=B  4=C  5=D  6=E  7=F#

## Pattern 7

This is labeled as "Pattern 7" because your 1st finger starts on the 7th scale degree.

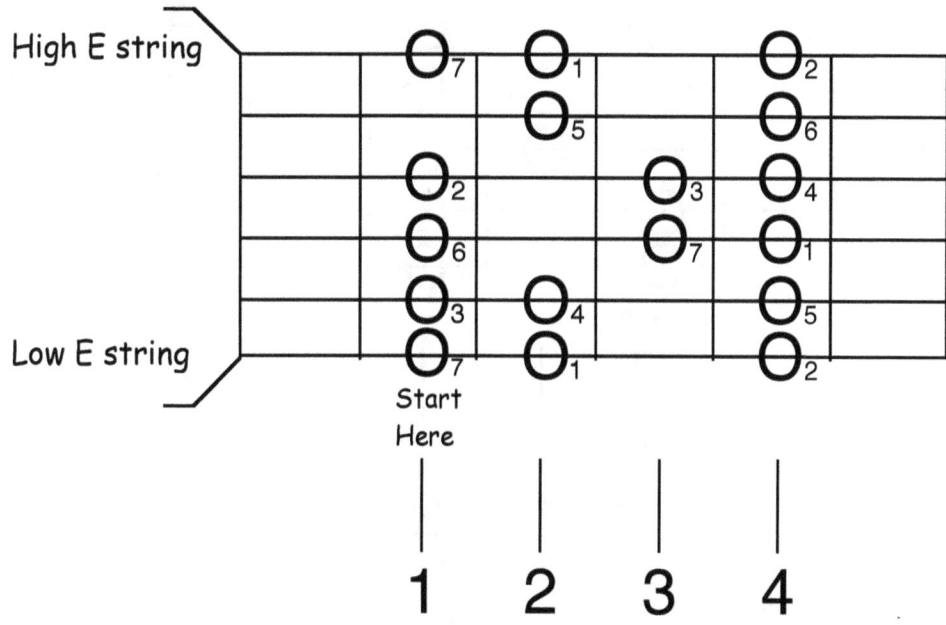

These larger numbers represent the left hand fingers that are used to play the notes on these particular frets (note that the thumb is not considered a finger on the left hand). So your left hand is coming across the neck of the guitar (bottom to top) using these fingers:

```
(end here)  High E string   1, 2, 4
                             2, 4
                            1, 3, 4
                            1, 3, 4
                            1, 2, 4
(start here) Low E string   1, 2, 4
```

# G "Major" & E "Pure Minor" Scale Shapes

# Pattern 1

This is labeled as "Pattern 1" because your 1st finger starts on the 1st scale degree.

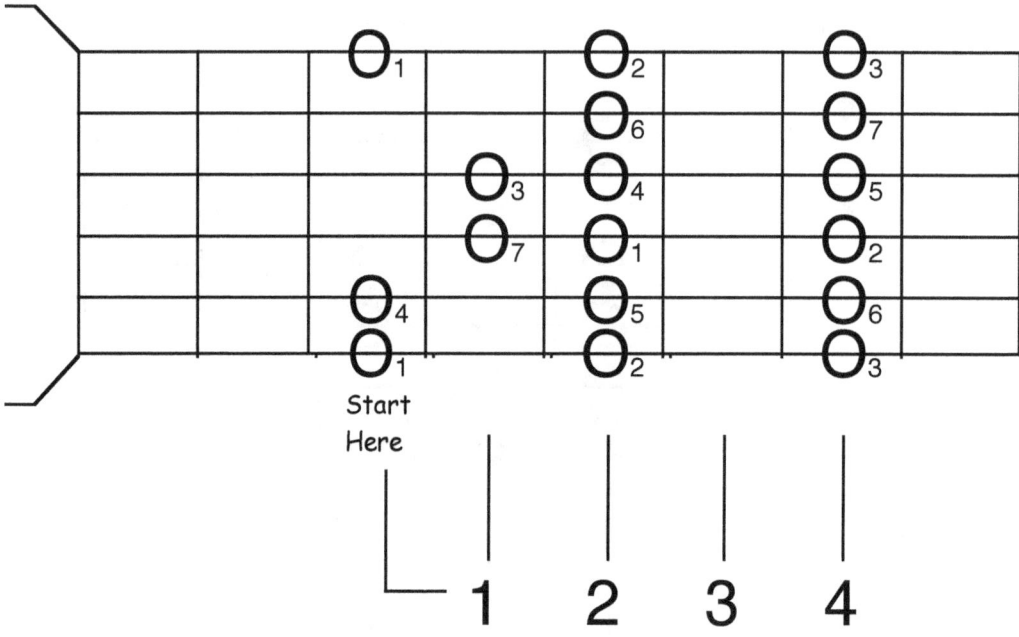

The first finger must "stretch" to play the notes on the third fret.

Note: when doing this, make sure that you still use your 2nd finger for the notes on the 5th fret and your 4th finger for the notes on the 7th fret.

If you have to move your left hand back and forth in order to use these fingerings, than do so. These fingerings will make "playing quickly" easier in the future and help to strengthen your left hand. Don't over do left hand stretches, particularly in the beginning. If you feel ANY fatigue, pain or strain in your left hand, fingers or arm, STOP and give your hand a rest! For beginners, these fingerings are awkward!

Also, remember to play these patterns backwards. Once you've gotten up to the last note on the high E string, come back down starting with your 4th finger (you don't need to repeat this top note).

# G "Major" & E "Pure Minor" Scale Shapes
## Pattern 2

This is labeled as "Pattern 2" because your 1st finger starts on the 2nd scale degree.

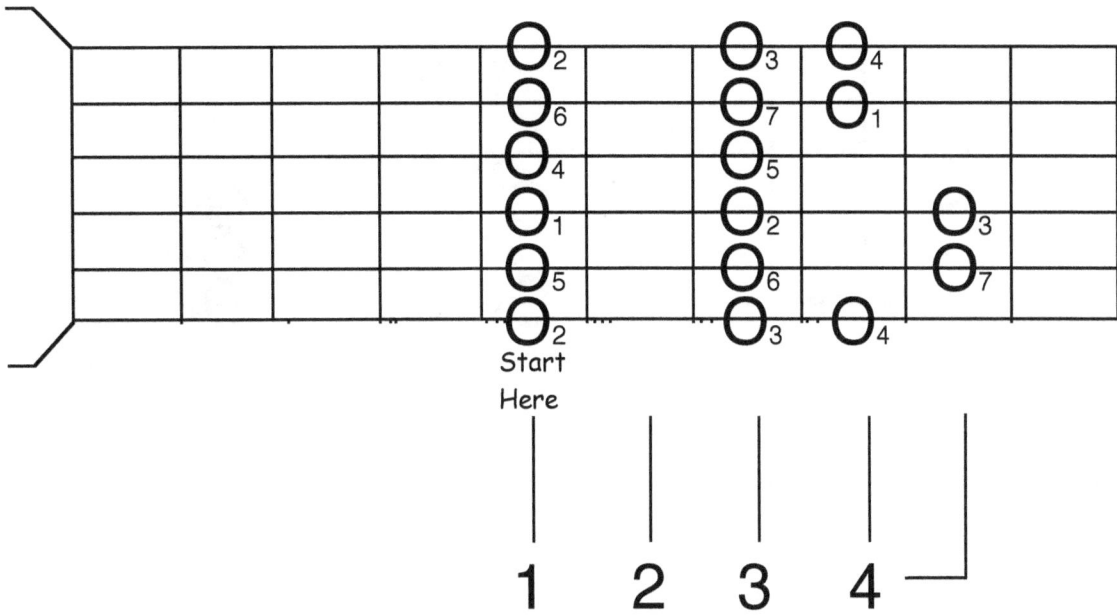

The 4th finger (your pinky) must "stretch" to play the notes on the 9th fret. Note: when doing this, make sure that you still use your 3rd finger for the notes on the 7th fret and your 1st finger for the notes on the 5th fret.

Again, if you have to move your left hand back and forth a little, in order to use these fingerings, than do so.

AND remember: Don't over-work your left hand!

Most guitars have dots on the neck. Use these dots to help keep your hand in place on the neck. It's very easy to slide out of position if you're not careful.

# G "Major" & E "Pure Minor" Scale Shapes

## Pattern 3

This is labeled as "Pattern 3" because your 1st finger starts on the 3rd scale degree.

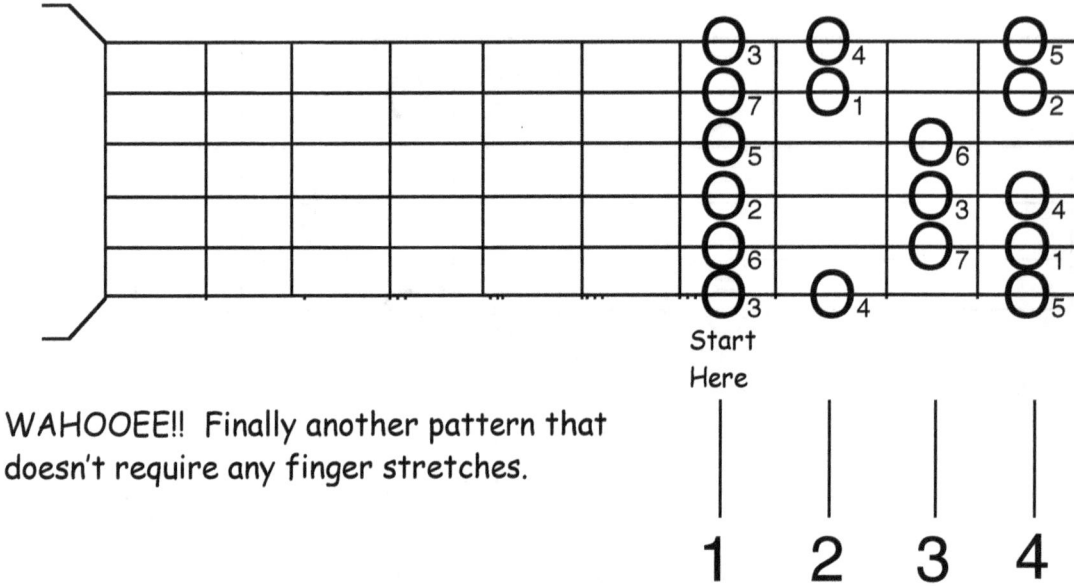

WAHOOEE!! Finally another pattern that doesn't require any finger stretches.

## Pattern 4

This is labeled as "Pattern 4" because your 1st finger starts on the 4th scale degree.

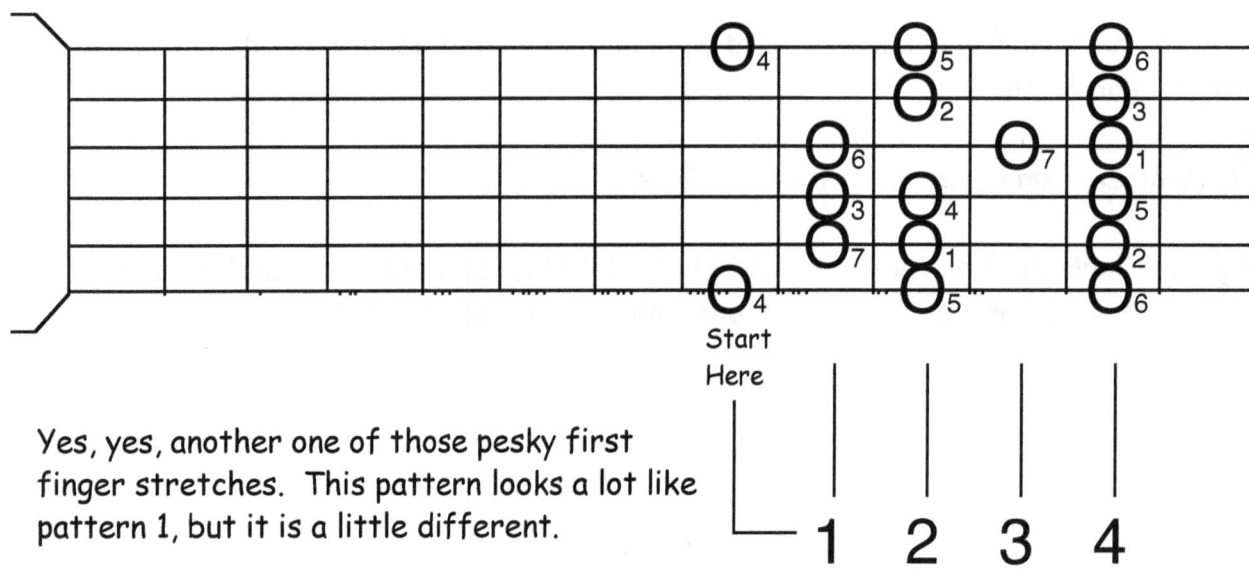

Yes, yes, another one of those pesky first finger stretches. This pattern looks a lot like pattern 1, but it is a little different.

# G "Major" & E "Pure Minor" Scale Shapes
# Pattern 5

This is labeled as "Pattern 5" because your 1st finger starts on the 5th scale degree.

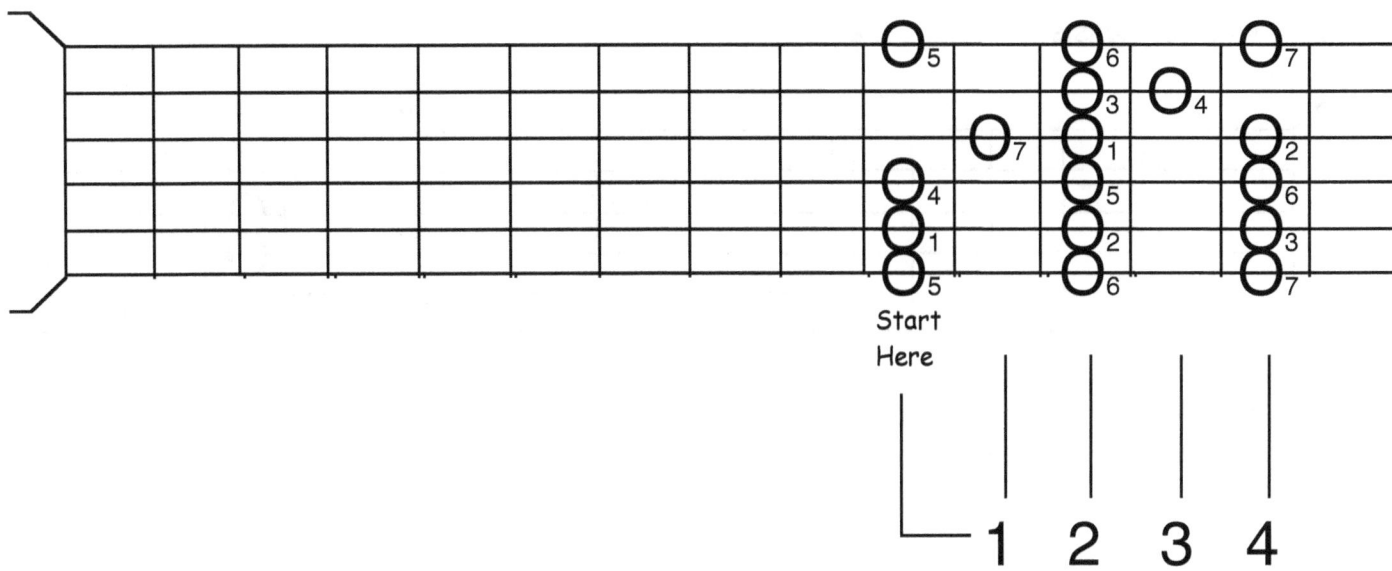

I know, I know, you thought that patterns 1, 2, & 4 were bad with the finger stretches...
...this one is "stretch-city"!! Luckily, in this key, pattern 5 occurs way up on the neck so the frets aren't that far apart.

Note: If you're playing an acoustic guitar or any guitar without a "cut-away" it may seem darn near impossible to reach these notes. You can always hike the guitar up on one knee and reach further around the neck with your left hand. Also, if you keep your left hand thumb further down on the back of the neck of the guitar, you will give your fingers more stretching room around front.

But, again, DON'T overdo practicing this pattern. You are asking your left hand to do things that it's just not used to, so go slow and monitor how your hand is feeling.

# G "Major" & E "Pure Minor" Scale Shapes
# Pattern 6

This is labeled as "Pattern 6" because your 1st finger starts on the 6th scale degree. (I realize that at this point you don't need or want this reminder, but there is something to be said for consistency... maybe.)

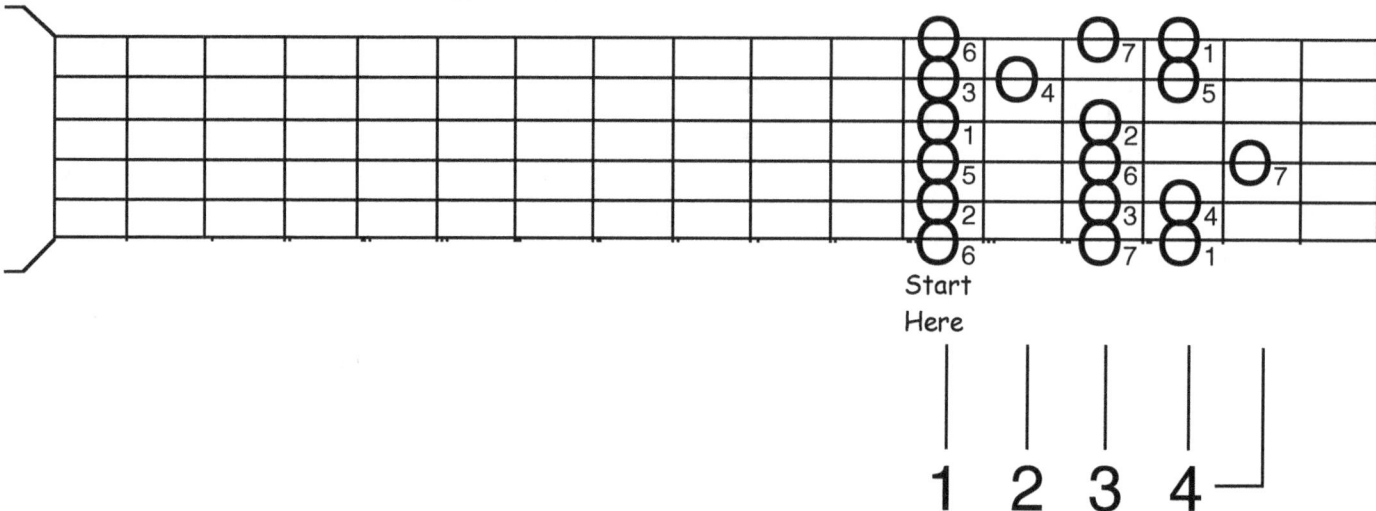

Pattern 6 is way up there. If you just can't reach these notes on the guitar that you have right now, run this pattern on a lower spot on the neck. But if there is any way humanly possible, run it way up there on the neck. Since the frets are so close together up there, playing up there is like playing a completely different instrument, and you're going to have to be comfortable with this part of the neck sooner or later.

Below is a diagram of pattern 6 with all of the other patterns in the G major/E natural minor scale combined.

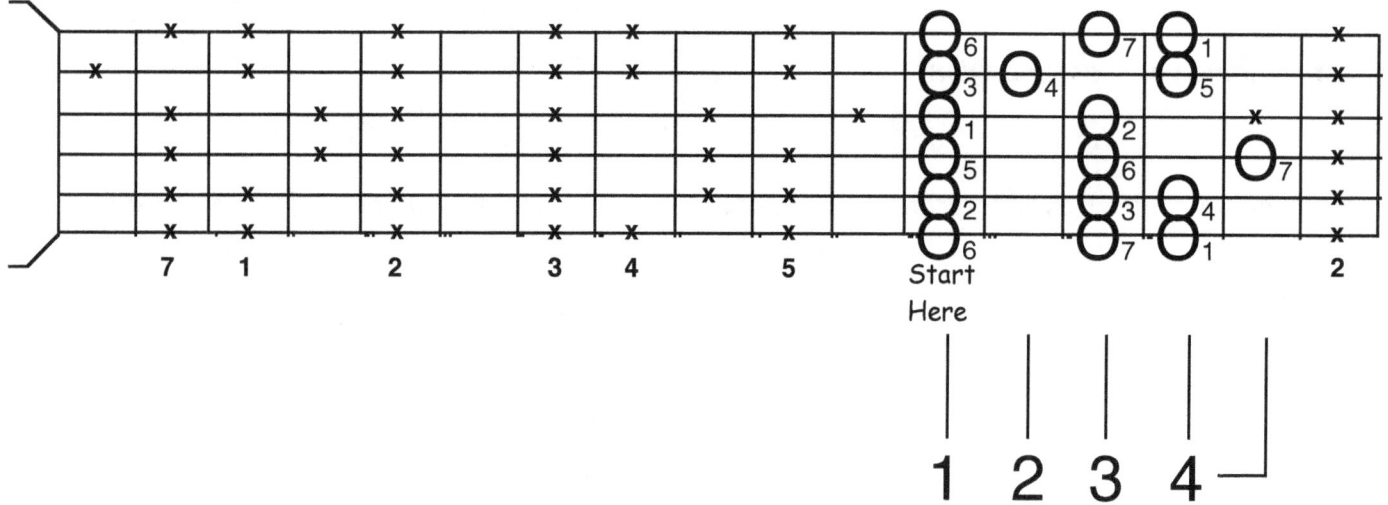

# WHAT'S NEXT?

Now you should get to the point where you can run all 7 major patterns forwards AND backwards without hesitation. You need to be able to play these patterns smoothly so that if someone wasn't looking at your hands, they couldn't tell that you were moving from one string to another. Don't telegraph how difficult it is to play the guitar. Start slowly and evenly. Always strive to play through these patterns evenly. Control is a large part of the game here.

Once you've memorized these 7 major patterns and can play them fairly smoothly, its time to work a bit on your right hand. In order to build up any kind of appreciable speed, you will need to be able to play these patterns with "alternate picking". What this means is that you now have to alternate your right hand pick motion with down strokes and up strokes: down, up, down, up, down, up, etc...

Make sure that you are using strict alternate picking. DON'T start each new string with a down stroke (this is called "slip picking" or "sweep picking"). Start each pattern with a down stroke and no matter what, whether you change strings or direction in the scale, use alternate picking. Do this with all 7 patterns. Play the entire pattern forwards and backwards without stopping, don't repeat the top note, and your last note should always end with a down stroke. At first this will slow you WAY down, but eventually you will be able to play twice as fast as you could with just down strokes!

After getting your "alternate picking" work started, you should be aware that when you solo, you'll want to be able to play anywhere on the neck. This means you'll have to tie all 7 of these patterns together into one huge pattern on the neck of the guitar. "Seeing" the major scale on the entire neck of the guitar, all at once, will take quite a while. Have patience and keep working at it... this may take... years..... gulp!

(of course, it may only take a few weeks... How much do you practice?)

# ...NOW WHAT?

OK, you've got all 7 major patterns down <u>and</u> you've committed them to memory <u>and</u> you're getting control over alternate picking. Now you're beginning to tie the 7 major patterns together on the neck so that you can ice-skate around, soloing anywhere on the neck, and still be in the key of G major/E minor. Obviously, as you are moving around on the neck, some of the fingerings will have to be changed in order to shift positions. But once you're in position, try to resume the "correct" fingerings. These fingerings will help you strengthen and develop all four left hand fingers equally (after a few years, you can use whatever fingers you like, but until then...).

To help you tie all of these patterns together, you should try soloing up and down the neck (from the headstock towards the body of the guitar and back) in the key of G, using only two adjacent strings. Work on knowing the scale along the length of each string. This will help solidify your knowledge of the major scale on the neck. And remember, most of the other scales will relate to these shapes, so you'll want to know this stuff really well!

**NOTE:** These patterns should become a daily warm-up routine. Before you start jamming and playing the "cool" stuff that you got off of the internet, run these patterns first. As more material is introduced in this book, add it to your daily warm-up. It might seem like a lot of stuff to play before you get to the latest counter-culture hit song, but in the long run, you will be leagues ahead of your neighbor who plays the same tunes and riffs over and over. And as you get better, this material will take less and less time to run through.

Now what about all the 11 other keys you've heard so much about? ....OK. Here's one of the great things about the guitar: When you go to another key, all of the 7 pattern shapes stay the same AND they come in the same order. They all just shift up or down the neck of the guitar. We learned all 7 patterns in the key of G major. If you wanted to play in the key of A major, the first thing you do is to look back at the chromatic scale and find out where the A is in relation to the G. You already know where the G is... its where all of the 1's are in the patterns that you've been learning. As you look at the chromatic scale you'll see that A is one whole step or 2 frets, up from the G. This means that you would have to shift all of the patterns "up" 2 frets (to the right). By doing this, pattern 7 would now be played on the 4th fret instead of the second fret. All of the other patterns come in the exact same order as they would in the key of G (just "up" 2 frets). So, pattern 7 on the 4th fret is followed by pattern 1 on the 5th fret, then pattern 2 on the 7th fret, then pattern 3 on the 9th fret, and so on.

Also, now that you've moved "up" 2 frets and pattern 7 is on the 4th fret, you've got room down on the 2nd fret for pattern 6. Remember that pattern 6 is always 2 frets below pattern 7. All of the patterns come in the same order, no matter what key you're in.

Getting back to figuring out where this A is in relationship to the G, chances are that you're not going to have a chromatic scale chart with you wherever you go, so the way to figure out how to play in any key is:

**Know where the letter names are along the entire low E string.**

And a good way to help you remember where all those notes are, is to know that all of the notes that have letter names are 2 frets apart on the neck...
EXCEPT: B to C and E to F.
... and , YES, this should all sound familiar. If it doesn't, and knowing the letter names on the low E string is a little sketchy to you, you should go back and review the Major Scale information provided just before all of the major scale patterns were given.

At this point you should try playing/soloing in the key of A major. Start with playing pattern 7 up on the 4th fret. After playing there for a while, see if you can slide up to pattern 1 in A major without getting lost. Notice that all of those friendly dots that you were using as guide posts will now all be different. You're going to have to divorce yourself from the dots that you've relied on and start to see the major patterns independently on the neck. Soon we'll start soloing back and forth between two different keys all over the neck. And eventually we'll deal with changing into many different keys within one tune!

# And Another Thing...

## ...What The Heck Is A "Mode"?

Alright, you've heard some of these funny names thrown around and you're wondering what you've been missing. The short and quick answer is: Nothing.

However, just to appease the curious, lets dispel the mystery once and for all. "Mode" is another word for "scale". Remember: music theory folk like to name and rename everything ... everything! If you play the G major scale starting with the 1st scale degree and ending with the 1st scale degree in a different octave, its given a name (Ionian). If you start with the 2nd scale degree and end with the 2nd scale degree in a different octave, its given another name (Dorian) and so on.

Since the major scale has 7 different scale degrees...
   ...that simple little G major scale now has 7 different names! (modes).
These 7 different names are:
   1: Ionian
   2: Dorian
   3: Phrygian
   4: Lydian
   5: Mixolydian
   6: Aeolian
   7: Locrian

Since the 7 letter names of the G major scale are: G A B C D E F#, this one major scale now can be referred to as:
   G Ionian (major scale)
   A Dorian
   B Phrygian
   C Lydian
   D Mixolydian
   E Aeolian (minor scale)
   F# Locrian

For the purposes of soloing, more than likely, you are not going to start on one scale degree and play straight up (or down) to the next octave. The only real use for these mode names is to describe or to specify a particular sound. Like which scale to use when soloing over a chord that, otherwise, could belong to two or more major scales.

For instance, lets say that you are given D minor as a chord to solo over.
Any minor chord can function as a 2, a 3, or a 6 chord in any major scale.
(***more on this and other chord-scale options later)

D minor can be a 2 chord in the key of C major
D minor can be a 3 chord in the key of Bb major
D minor can be a 6 chord in the key of F major
(I'll explain more about how to figure out these keys in the chapter on chords)

This means that if you are given a D minor chord to solo over, you can play the C major scale, the Bb major scale, or the F major scale.

D minor can be a 2 chord in the key of C major.........D Dorian = C Major
D minor can be a 3 chord in the key of Bb major......D Phrygian = Bb Major
D minor can be a 6 chord in the key of F major........D Aeolian = F Major

As a soloist, it is up to you to choose what sound (scale/mode) to play over this D minor chord. If, however, the composer wants you to play a specific sound (scale/mode) over the D minor, they may write "dorian" next to the chord. All this means is that they want you to think of the D as a 2 chord and solo using the C major scale sound.

This is one of the most common ways that those funny "mode" names are used. Of course, as an improviser, you may veto this request from the composer and play whatever you want.... as long as you can make good music.

The other most common way that these names are used is when describing what sound (scale) was used by a soloist (for transcription purposes). So you'll see these names being thrown about a lot in magazines that have transcriptions of various solos.

But remember, all of these names are just referring to different starting places within the major scale. Your main goal should be knowing the major scale through and through... all over the neck. Don't think that you are missing out because someone wants to know if you can play the C lydian scale. C lydian is the same thing as the G major scale starting on the C (the 4th pitch)!! When you are soloing in G major, you are simultaneously using all of these "modes".

If you want to throw these names around, you can learn them, but the bottom line is:

## KNOW THE MAJOR SCALE ON THE ENTIRE NECK!!

# THE PENTATONIC SCALE

### WHAT?!?

Another scale?.... yup. Only you will grow to love this scale even more than the major scale. With the pentatonic scale, there are fewer patterns to learn, the patterns use less notes, <u>and</u> they sound great!

(yeah, yeah, I'm not much of a salesman.... but you really will like this scale)

AND, like almost all of the scales in this book, I've related them back to the 7 major patterns that you worked so hard to learn. **The Major Method is a somewhat unorthodox approach to learning the scales. However, it's quicker, it's easier, and it's exactly the same information.**

BUT FIRST... a thumb-nail sketch of where this scale came from. This scale pretty much changed the sound of "Western" music (and, no I don't mean country western music).

Unfortunately, this scale and its use came out of one of the uglier chapters in the US history book. During slavery, many African people were forced to come to the US. There were nations and communities in South Africa where the predominant musical scale/tonality had 5 notes to the octave. These notes included pitches that were "in between" the scale pitches of the Western major scale construct. Today these notes are referred to as "blue" notes and are often played by bending or sliding notes up or down.

Given the enormity of Human ingenuity and the Human spirit (and in a desire to recapture the spirit of "Home" ) this Western musical system was adapted by these enslaved people, to create a sound that was more familiar. Since the predominant scale in the Western system was the 7 note major scale and a 5 note sound was desired, two notes needed to be eliminated.

**NOTE:** The pentatonic sound was a sound unto itself, so its introduction and use had less to do with subtracting notes from the major scale and had more to do with simply trying to recreate a familiar sound. This perspective of "eliminating" 2 notes from the major scale in order to come up with the pentatonic scale is a way to learn the "sound/shapes" on the neck of the guitar (again, relating them back to the major scale patterns that you've learned). It is a quick, functional approach. It builds on what you've already learned. It is... (sound the trumpets here) ...the "Major Method".

The major scale's two smallest intervals are:

1) The half step that occurs between the 3rd to 4th scale degrees.
2) The half step that occurs between the 7th to 1st scale degrees.
   *If this "scale degree" stuff doesn't sound familiar, review the "major scale" written material given earlier in this book.

So both the 4th and 7th pitches of the major scale were eliminated in order to create the pentatonic scale ("penta" means five, so the "pentatonic" scale has 5 notes).

In this way, the G major pentatonic scale comes from...
...the G major scale:

G major scale:................ G  A  B  C  D  E  F#
                              1  2  3  4  5  6  7
G major pentatonic scale: G  A  B     D  E

This scale and its sound gave birth to the Blues which, in turn, gave birth to Jazz, Rock, R&B, and many of the other sounds that we hear on "popular" radio today. It even greatly affected the classical world through Debussy, Ravel and others.

The history of the pentatonic scale is one of the reasons why Jazz and Blues are sometimes referred to as African-American art forms. It is important to be familiar with the history and rich past of any art form that you pursue. Most importantly, however, one must realize that this music is a Human art form and a celebration of Humanity, open to ALL who love great music and art.

OK, back to the pentatonic scale!

Remember, since we now only have 5 notes in this scale, we're only going to have 5 patterns to learn across the neck of the guitar. And while it is tempting to just play the major scale and try to eliminate the 4's and the 7's on the fly, it is much easier if you "see" the pentatonic patterns separately at first and get a solid fix on these shapes.

Even though there will be times when you can play the pentatonic scale and you "can't" play the major scale, it is important to be able to see the major scale patterns underneath these patterns as you play them. There *are* instances when you will want to go back and forth between the major patterns and the pentatonic patterns...
Tired of reading?
Want to start playing? ...OK, OK. Here, now are the pentatonic patterns:

# G "Major" Pentatonic Scale Shapes
## Pattern 7

The small numbers represent the Major Pentatonic scale pitches:
1=G  2=A  3=B  5=D  6=E

This is labeled as Pattern "7" because IF you used your 1st finger on the low E string, it would start on the 7th scale degree. BUT remember: there are no 7's in the pentatonics, so you start this pattern with your 2nd finger.

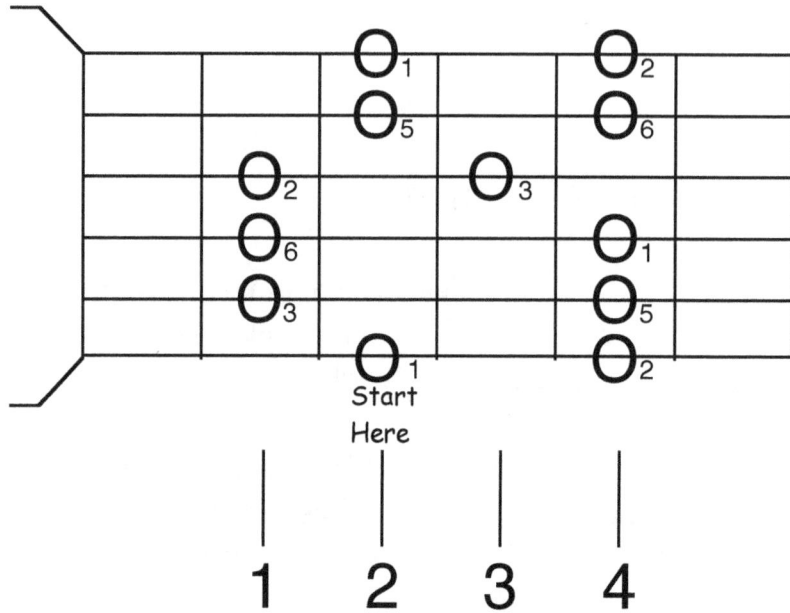

These larger numbers represent the left hand fingers that are used to play the notes on these particular frets (as with the major patterns, the thumb is not considered a finger on the left hand). The small numbers represent the scale degrees of the pentatonic scale **as they relate to the major scale.** Notice that there are no 4's or 7's in the diagram above. The diagram below shows how the pentatonic scale lives on top of the major scale.

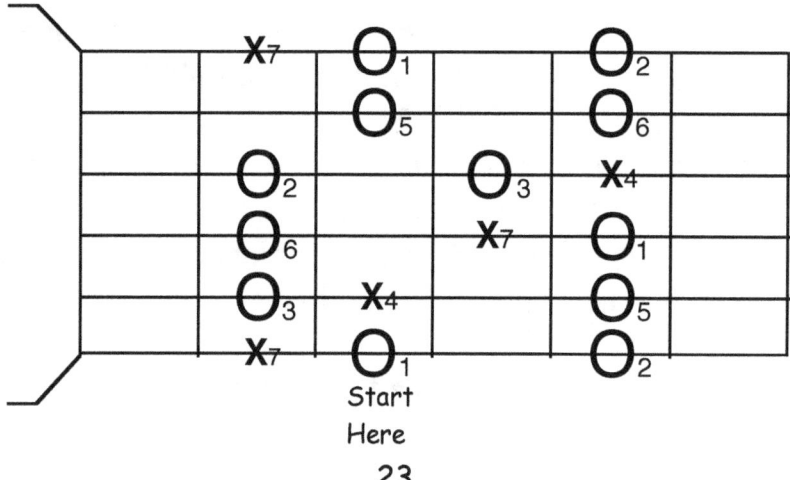

# G Major Pentatonic Scale Shapes
## Pattern "1 & 2 Combined"

This is labeled as Pattern "1 & 2 Combined" because it is the pentatonic pattern that combines the major scale patterns 1 & 2 (not a great name, but a descriptive name).

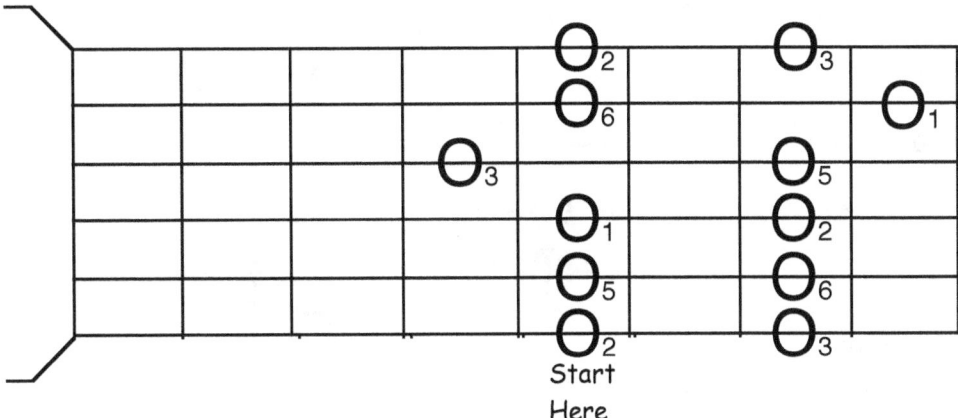

OK, here's the 1st scale pattern where you can choose your own fingering. There's no standard fingering for this pattern because it's such a strange shape. It's basically straight down the 5th fret and straight down the 7th fret with one note out on one side and one note out on the other side. If you have to move your left hand back and forth in order to play this pattern comfortably, than go ahead. BUT don't just use one finger to get through this pattern! Use primarily your 1st and 3rd fingers or your 2nd and 4th fingers.

While the major scale patterns overlap and dove-tail with each other, the pentatonic patterns all butt up against each other and share a wall of notes (like a jigsaw puzzle). The diagram below shows how the "1 & 2 Combined" pattern lives next to the "7" pattern.

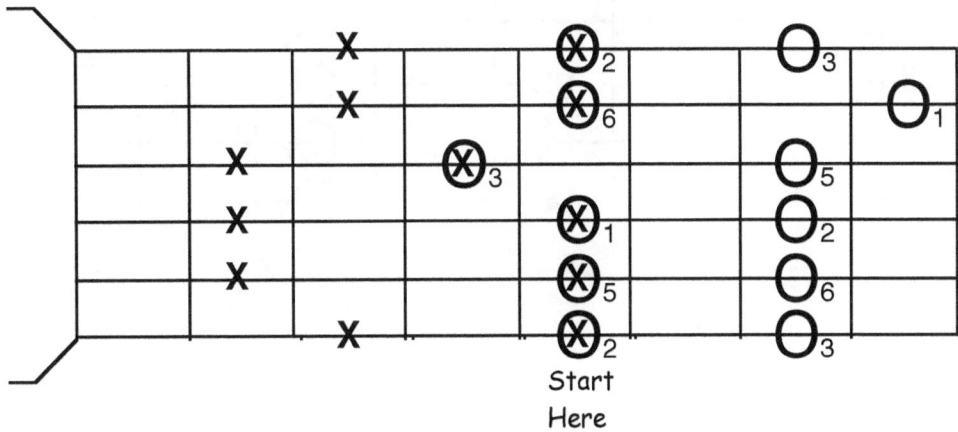

24

# Major vs Pentatonic Adjacent Scale Shapes

I've included this page just for clarification of the difference between how the major scale patterns "overlap" and the pentatonic patterns "butt up against" each other. Below are comparisons of how the major scale patterns 7 and 1 dove-tail, and how the pentatonic scale patterns 7 and 1 & 2 Combined share a wall of notes.

## Major Patterns 7 & 1

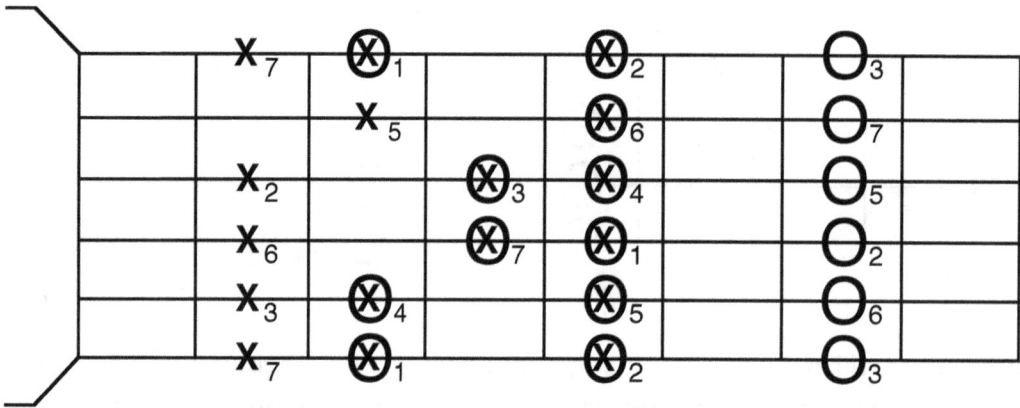

## Pentatonic Patterns 7 and "1 & 2 Combined"

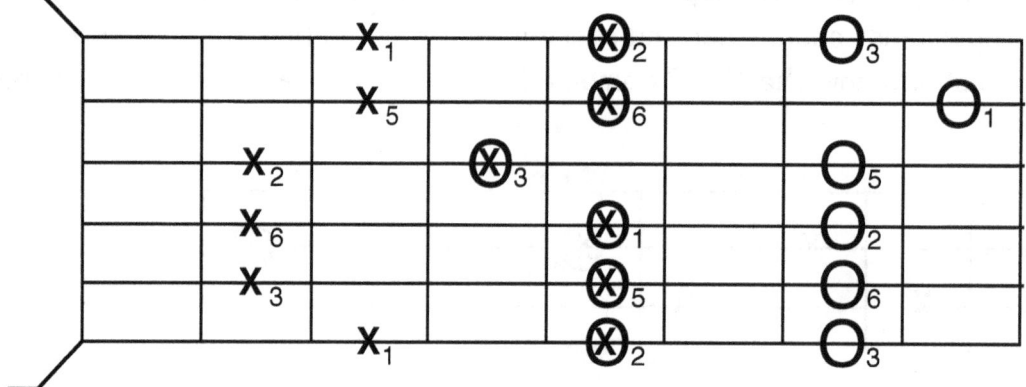

# G "Major" Pentatonic Scale Shapes

OK, enough discussion, here are the rest of the pentatonic patterns. As with all of these diagrams, the big numbers represent which of your left hand fingers you use, and the little numbers represent the scale degrees as they relate to the major scale.

## Pattern 3

This is labeled as "Pattern 3" because it starts with the... 3rd scale degree!

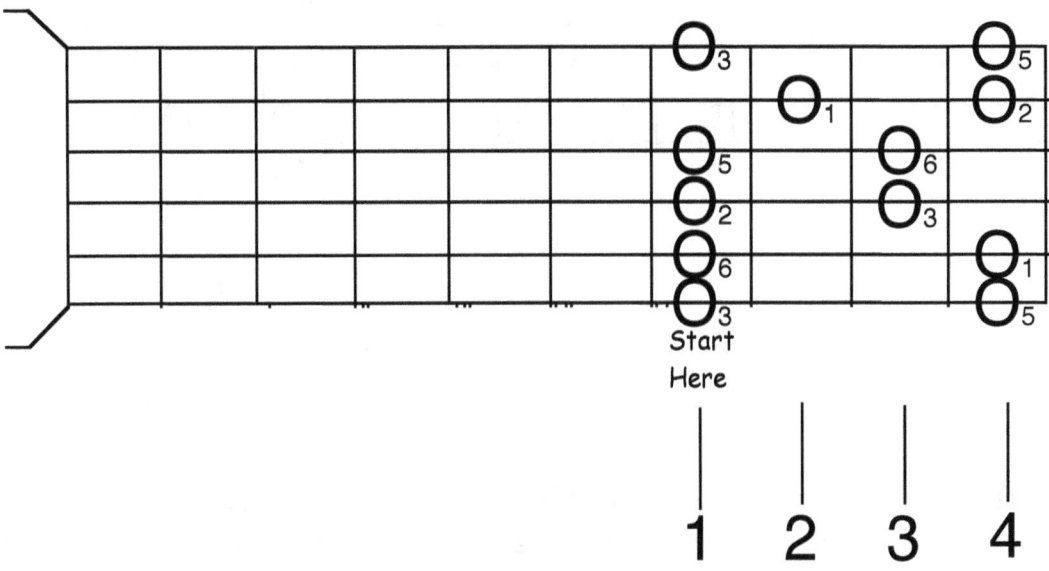

## Pattern "4 & 5 Combined"

Yes, this pattern also starts with your 2nd finger (like pattern 7).

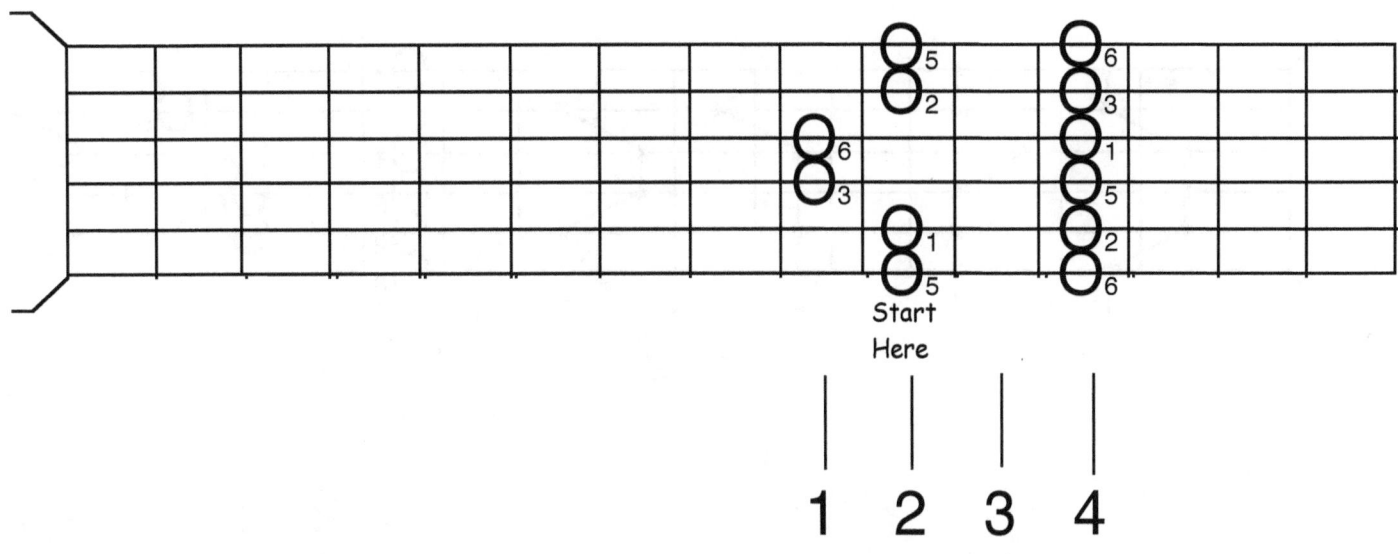

# G "Major" Pentatonic Scale Shapes
## Pattern 6

This pattern seems to be the favorite pattern of most young aspiring guitar players. It may have something to do with how comfortably it fits into the left hand. HOWEVER, one should strive to be equally comfortable with ALL of the patterns.

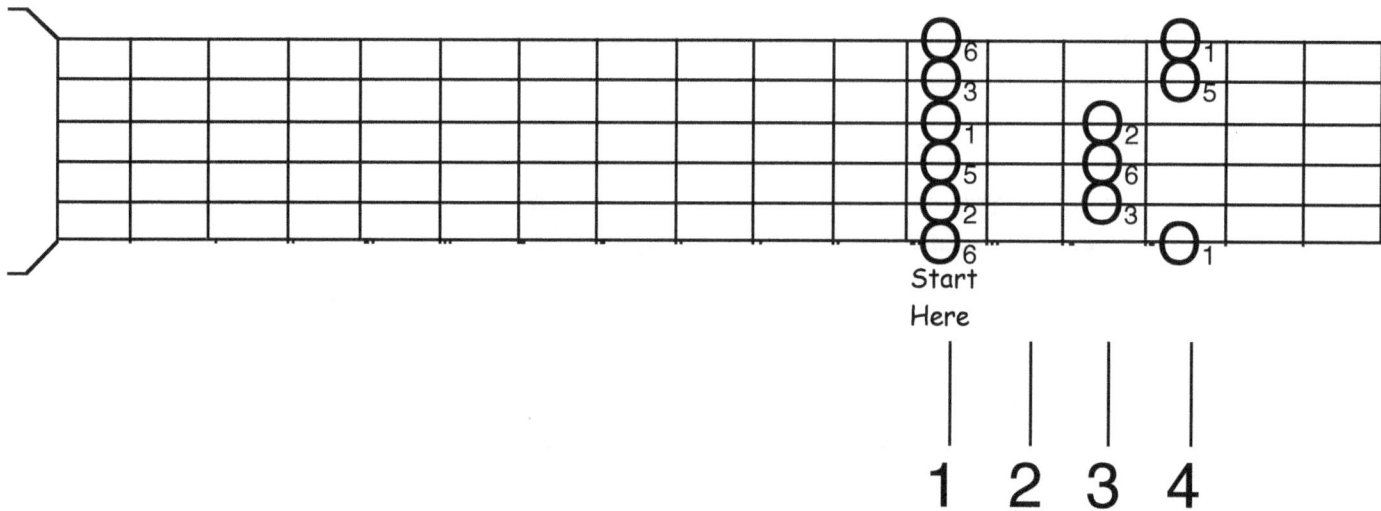

Now, here is a view of the entire neck of the guitar in G major pentatonic. I have connected the notes of the other pentatonic shapes with lines to make it easier to see the patterns and how they relate to each other. Notice how the patterns begin to repeat themselves once you get up high enough. This is ALWAYS the order of the pentatonic patterns. Even when we change keys, the shapes stay the same and they come in the same order. They all just slide "up" or "down" on the neck (more on this later).

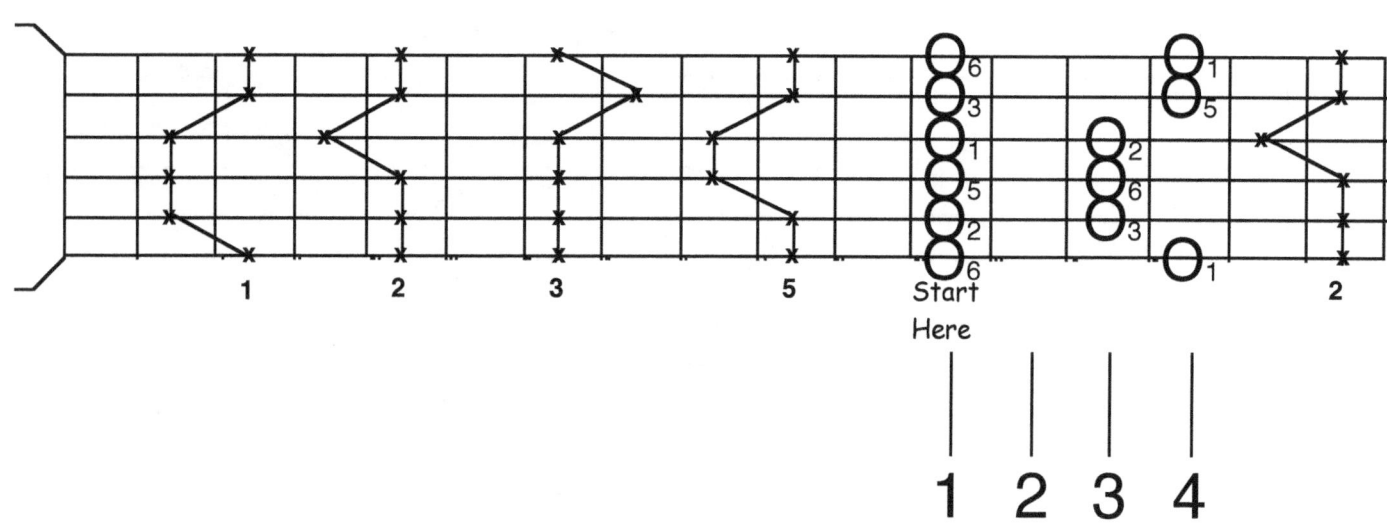

# NAME GAME

Once again you will have to memorize all 5 of these pentatonic patterns and tie them together on the neck so that it becomes one huge pattern. This scale, like the major scale, has more than one name. It too has a major name and a minor name:

1) The major pentatonic name comes from whatever note is the "1" of the scale. So these pentatonic patterns that you've learned are the G major pentatonic scale (because all of the 1's are G's).

2) The minor pentatonic name comes from whatever note is the "6" of the scale. So these pentatonic patterns that you've learned are also the E minor pentatonic scale (because all of the 6's are E's).

These pentatonic patterns ALSO have a third name (...a rose by any other name... ...hmmmm). If you add one more optional note to the pentatonic patterns, you have:

3) The Blues scale. This extra note has many names (b5, #11, b3, #9, blue note, etc...). None of this really matters. What matters is that you know where this note is and you are able to hear how this note can be used. The Blues scale is just like the minor pentatonic scale, in that the Blues scale name comes from whatever note is the "6" of the scale. **So the Blues scale and the minor pentatonic scale are exactly the same... EXCEPT** the Blues scale has this one extra note that we haven't gone over yet. Because of the "Major Method" numbering system, this new note functions as a b3. This note traditionally has been used as a passing note (a note that you don't hang out on for too long when you're soloing). HOWEVER, we're getting into pretty subjective territory here, and you should use this note as much or as little as you want. After all, this is about you finding your own voice on the guitar.

Keep in mind that all of the pattern numbers (the labels that we've given these scale diagrams) are NOT universal. Every guitar teacher and theoretician has a different name, a different number, a different way of carving up the neck of the guitar, a different approach to cooking, and a different set of fingerprints. You could call pattern 7 the "red" pattern, and pattern 3 the "iron" pattern. What we call these shapes only matters in how the names help us to organize these concepts in our mind so that we can learn them more efficiently and thoroughly. All of the different names that you may come across deal with these same shapes. They may show you only part of them, introduce them in a different order, or tie them together in different ways, but ultimately, these shapes are the language that all guitar players use.

So... DON'T get into arguments with your friends about what to call the G major scale pattern that occurs on the 7th fret of the guitar. There will be no winners here and you both will have gotten way off track from what's really important.... ...MAKING MUSIC! Now, lets add this one note to the pentatonic patterns, so you'll have another scale (the Blues scale) under your belt.

# E Blues Scale Shapes
## Pattern 7

The small numbers represent the Major/Minor Pentatonic scale pitches:
1=G  2=A  b3=Bb  3=B  5=D  6=E

This is labeled as Pattern "7" because IF you used your 1st finger on the low E string, it would start on the 7th scale degree. BUT remember: there are no 7's in the pentatonics or Blues, so you start this pattern with your 2nd finger. I have used the @ symbol to represent the b3 or "blue note"... (that's where it's @!)

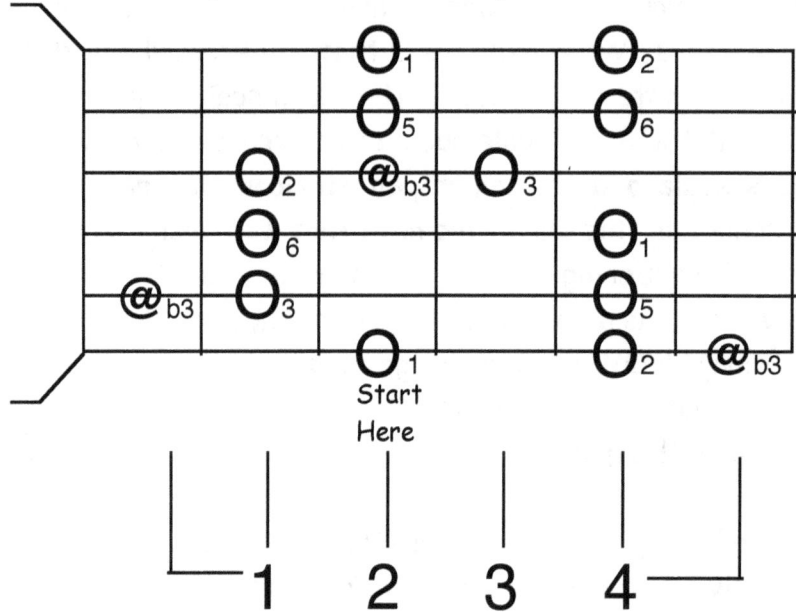

The b3 on the 1st fret of the A string is the same note as the one on the 6th fret of the low E string. I have included them both because when you're soloing, you will need to know where all of the available notes are under your fingers. As you begin this pattern (ascending from the low E string towards the high E string), DON'T use the b3 on the low E string. Use the b3 that is on the A string (on the left). Stretch your 1st finger out to play it and then slide your 1st finger in to also play the natural 3 in the next fret. On your way back, DON'T use the b3 on the A string. Use the b3 on the low E string (on the right). Stretch your little finger out to play it and then slide your little finger in to also play the 2 in the next fret.

29

# You Call That A Reason?

There is a reason for using your 1st finger to grab the b3 and slide it in to the natural 3 on the way "up" the strings and for using your little finger to grab the b3 and slide it in to the natural 3 on the way "down" the strings. The reason is that the muscles in our hands are stronger at pulling in (like making a fist) than at pushing out (like making... a.... making... a... an open hand with spread fingers!). So, in theory, you won't tax your hand as much if you use your 1st finger to play the b3 on the A string and pull this same finger in for the natural 3 and if you use your little finger to play the b3 on the low E and pull this same finger in again for the 2 (please, no "pull my finger" jokes).

Whenever learning something new, it helps if there is consistent repetition. So for all of these blues patterns, be consistent and play all of the blue notes on the left as you ascend and all of the blue notes on the right as you descend. By doing it one way consistently, you'll help to establish a knowledge of where these notes are. This way of playing both of the "blue" notes, primarily applies to when you are running the scales in practice. When you are on stage soloing, you can use whatever finger you like...
... (OK, insert "finger" joke here).

REMEMBER: The real objective is to know where all of the available notes are and to make sure that your hand is used to getting to all of these notes.


Alright, already!....


Here are the rest of the Blues patterns....

# E Blues Scale Shapes
# Pattern "1 & 2 Combined"

Don't get hung up on what to call this pattern, just run it and get to know it.

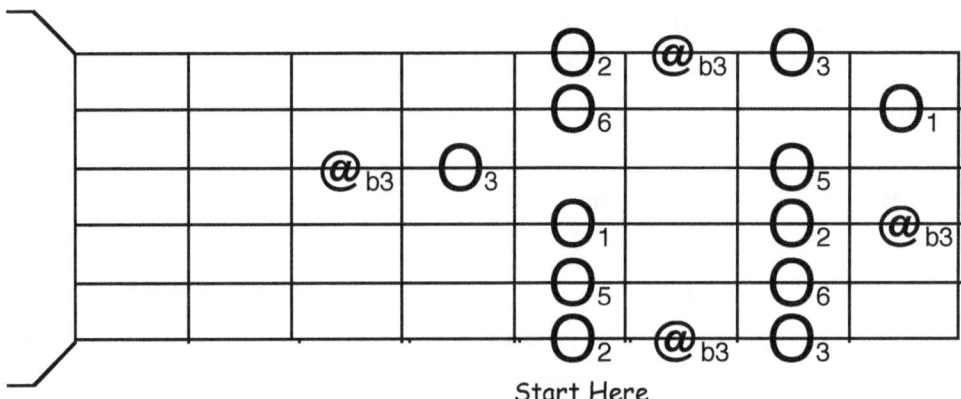

Start Here

This is probably the weirdest of the Blues patterns... and, YES, it is a ridiculous stretch to play the b3 on the G string (on the way "up"), but its not so bad when you grab the b3 on the D string on the way "down". You will have to move your left hand back and forth in order to play this pattern comfortably....

....But still grab the b3 on the left (with your 1st finger) on the way "up" and slide it in to the natural 3. Grab the b3 on the right (with your little finger) on the way "down" and slide it in to the 2.

When you're soloing you can use whichever "blue note/b3" you desire. But if you get into the habit of playing both of these stretches when you're practicing the scale, then you'll have them both at the ready when you're on the gig and there just isn't enough time to think about where that other %!#@!*ing blue note lives.

# E Blues Scale Shapes

Remember, grab the b3 on the left (with your 1st finger) on the way "up" and slide it in to the natural 3. Grab the b3 on the right (with your little finger) on the way "down" and slide it in to the 2.

## Pattern 3

## Pattern "4 & 5 Combined"

And again: b3 on the left on the way "up"....b3 on the right on the way down.

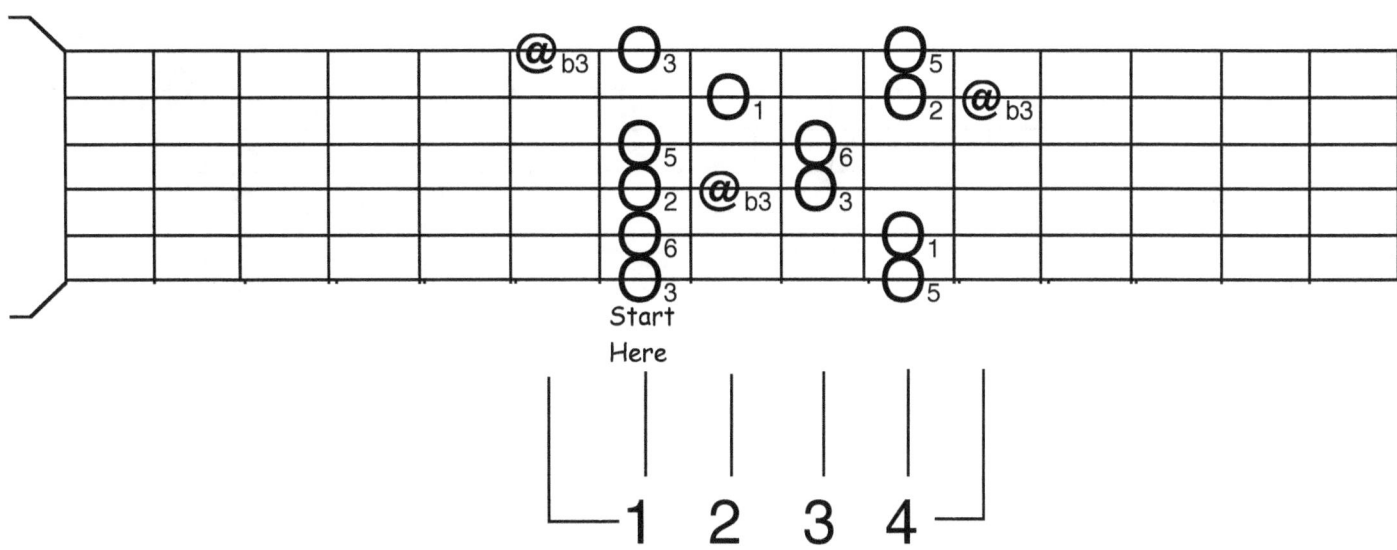

# E Blues Scale Shapes
## Pattern 6

Hey! Here's a pattern that doesn't have any finger stretches!! ....maybe this is why this is one of the favorite patterns of so many guitarists. Also, since this pattern starts on the 6th scale degree, it is the Blues' namesake (the name comes from the 6th scale degree).

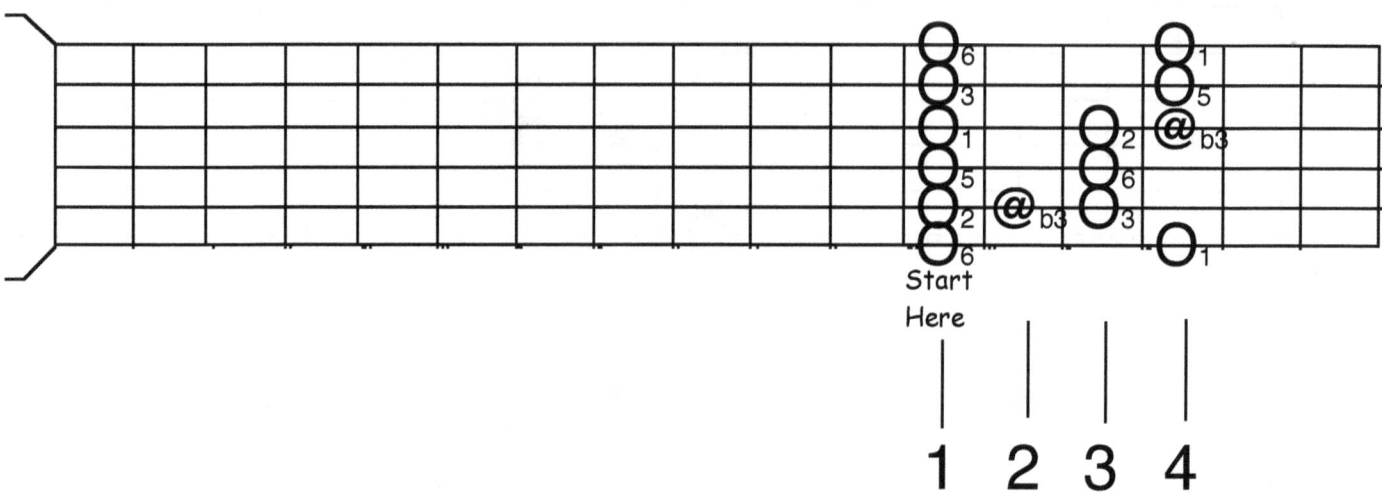

Now, here is a view of the entire neck of the guitar for the E Blues. I have connected most of the notes of the other Blues shapes with lines to make it easier to see the patterns and how they relate to each other. Notice how the patterns begin to repeat themselves once you get up high enough on the neck. This is ALWAYS the order of the Blues patterns.

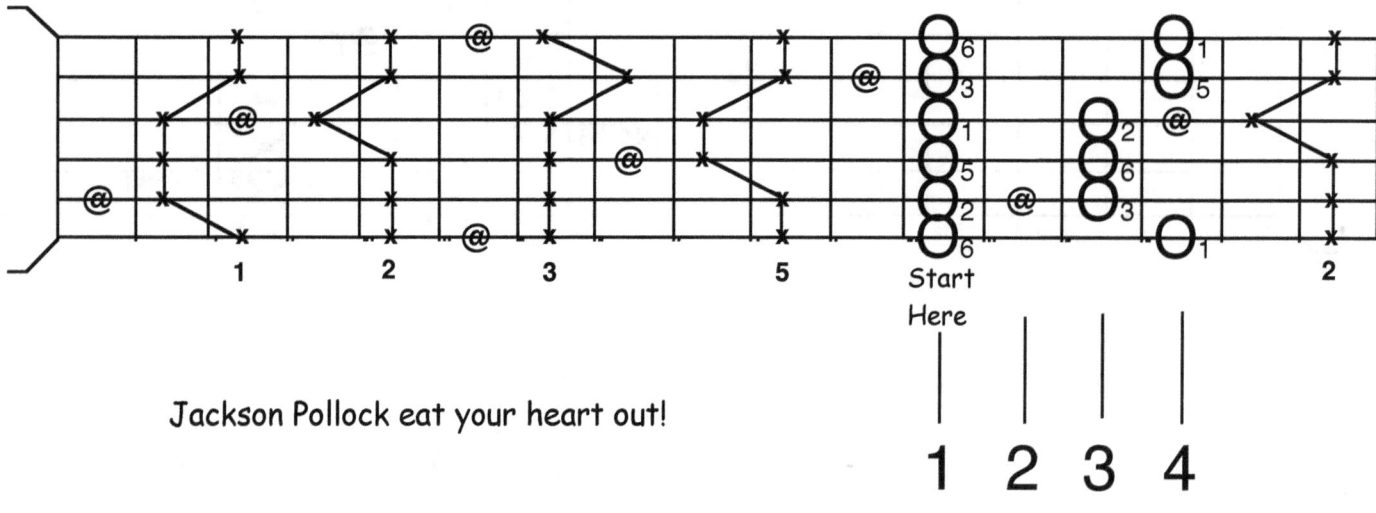

Jackson Pollock eat your heart out!

33

# WHAT ABOUT CHORDS?

Chords all come from the scales. You can build a chord on any one of the notes in a scale. The note that you choose to build a chord on is called the "root" of the chord. And since the major scale has 7 different notes in it, it also has 7 different chords within it.

We've been working with the key of G major, so lets figure out what chords are in the key of G major. These chords all come from the G major scale, so if you're writing a tune in the key of G major, these chords will all basically fit (most tunes do not use all of the chords in a key, they just use some of them). The 7 notes in the key of G major are:

```
G  A  B  C  D  E  F#
1  2  3  4  5  6  7
```

There are two basic types of chords that are used today.
        1. Triads (chords that use only 3 different notes as a base: triadic)
        2. Sevenths (chords that use 4 different notes as a base: quartal)

Whether you are using triadic (3 note) harmony or quartal (4 note) harmony, all chords are built in 3rds. This means that a chord is made up of every other note from the root (the root is the starting note), until you have your 3 or 4 notes (chord tones).

So if you start with the G (the 1 chord... G is now the root),
The 3 note chord would be spelled: G, B, D.
The 4 note chord would be spelled: G, B, D, F#

If you start with the A (the 2 chord... A is now the root):
The 3 note chord would be spelled: A, C, E.
The 4 note chord would be spelled: A, C, E, G.

The three notes of a triad are referred to as:
1. the "root"
2. the "third"
3. the "fifth"

The four notes of a seventh chord are referred to as:
1. the "root"
2. the "third"
3. the "fifth"
4. the "seventh"

So in the three note G chord, the G is the root, the B is the third, and the D is the fifth. In the four note G chord, the G is the root, the B is the third, the D is the fifth, and the F# is the seventh. Remember that each of the 7 notes of the major scale can have a chord built on it. Each of these 7 chords that come from the major scale have their own sound or their own "tonality". The words that are used to describe these tonalities are as follows:

| TRIAD TONALITY | SEVENTH TONALITY |
| --- | --- |
| 1 Chord= Major | 1 Chord= Major 7 |
| 2 Chord= Minor | 2 Chord= Minor 7 |
| 3 Chord= Minor | 3 Chord= Minor 7 |
| 4 Chord= Major | 4 Chord= Major 7 |
| 5 Chord= Major | 5 Chord= Dominant 7 |
| 6 Chord= Minor | 6 Chord= Minor 7 |
| 7 Chord= Minor b5 or Diminished | 7 Chord= Minor 7 b5 or Half Diminished |

# THREE-NOTE CHORDS

One of the most common ways to play triad harmony on the guitar is with what are called "barre chords". These chords are used all over the place in today's "popular" music (and not-so-popular music). These chords are popular because they have movable forms, which is to say that once your hand is in position, you can pretty much slide the form around on the neck of the guitar and begin to play tunes.

There are at least two drawbacks to using barre chords:
1. There isn't a barre chord for the "7 chord" of the major scale.
2. At first, its kind of hard to get a good sound out of these barre chords.

**NOTE:** Barre chords require a fair amount of strength in your left hand. At first, don't practice these chords for hours on end. You'll run the risk of hurting your hand. If you start to feel ANY strain or pain in your left hand, wrist, or forearm, STOP. Go off and grab a soda or do something else for a little while. Give your hand a chance to recover. Don't go by that old saying; "No pain, no gain", it's full of bologna! If you're feeling strain or pain, then your body is telling you to give it a rest. So... GIVE IT A REST!!

## There are basically two types of barre chords:
1. The type that has the "root" on the low E string.
2. The type that has the "root" on the A string (the 5th string).

Again, the "root" of a chord is the letter name that the chord is built on. So the root of a G major chord is the G. The root of an A minor chord is the A. These roots are frequently (but not always) the lowest note in the chord. When the root is the lowest note of the chord, the chord is said to be in "root position". All of the following barre chord examples are in "root position".

## MORE NOTES:

Because there isn't a "7 chord" in barre chord land, AND the "7 chord" is the only triad tonality that isn't a major or minor chord, you'll only have to learn major voicings and minor voicings for the barre chords.

The 1st set of barre chords that we'll look at is the "root on the low E" barre chords. These chords use all 6 strings and will require a good deal of strength in the left hand as well as a good dose of patience....

The 2nd set of barre chords will be the "root on the A" barre chords. With the muffling of the low E string and the partial barring of the 3rd finger for the major type in this category, these chords will have their own set of difficulties....

There are other ways of playing triads. Some of these ways include "open chords" ("folk chords") which use open strings as part of their sound. These chords are sometimes used just as much as barre chords. Also one can opt to play the 3 notes of the triad anywhere on the neck of the guitar. I like this option, but it tends to be very quiet and not as full sounding.

Today, many heavier rock bands play only the bottom 2 or 3 strings of the barre chords. When doing this, you're only playing the root and fifth of the chord. These chords are often refered to as "5 chords" (not to be confused with the chord that is built on the 5th scale degree). These chords are often written in charts like this:
$G^5$, $C^5$, or $D^5$.

Also, today, many bands "de-tune" their low E string to a "D". This enables them to play a barre-type "5 chord" with only one finger barred across the low 3 strings (making it super easy to play fast parallel chord passages). Sometimes bands will de-tune their whole guitar down a whole step. All of these options can give the guitar a deeper, heavier sound.... but right now we're going to focus on the basic barre chords with the standard tuning!!

# ROOT ON THE LOW "E"
## BARRE CHORD VOICINGS

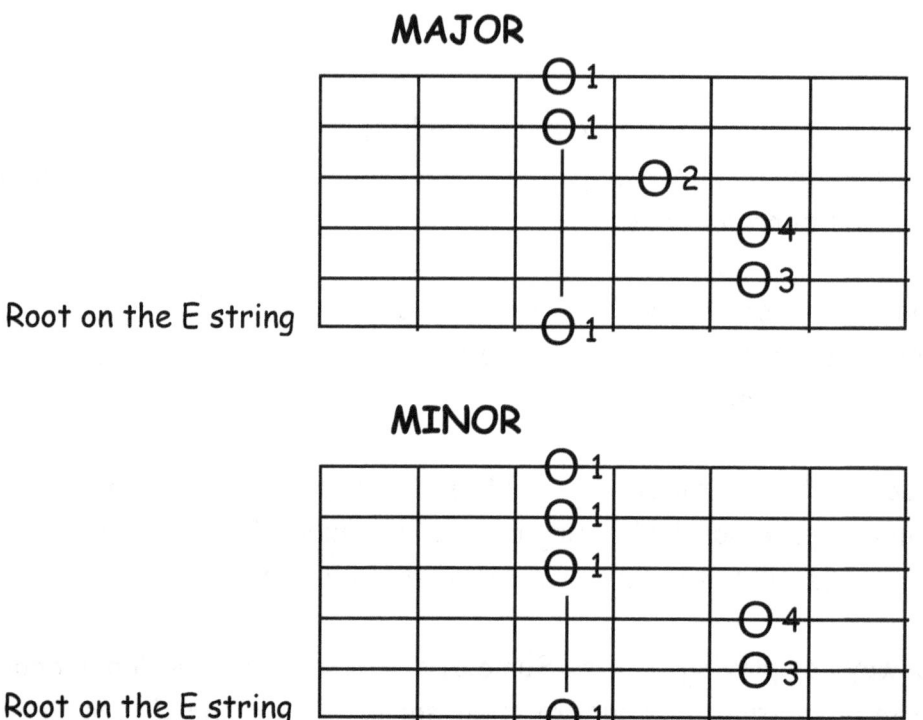

The numbers that you see on these diagrams represent each of the left hand fingers that are used to play these notes. As you've noticed, your 1st finger is playing more than one note. Your 1st finger has to "barre" across the neck of the guitar, clamping down on all 6 strings in order to play these chords (hence the name: barre chords).

The trick of playing these chords well, lies in your ability to keep your 1st finger straight while keeping your other fingers curved and onto their tips. Everyone's 1st finger is a bit different, so you may have to experiment with raising or lowering the position of your 1st finger across the neck, in order to get a good, clean sound out of these chords. You may want to roll your 1st finger back onto its side where there is more of a bony surface and less of a puffy, fleshy-type surface. While keeping this 1st finger straight, you'll also need to keep the other fingers arched in a nice high curve, coming down only on their tips. This will help in getting a clean sound on all of the notes without muffling the notes on the adjacent strings.

# ROOT ON THE "A"
## BARRE CHORD VOICINGS

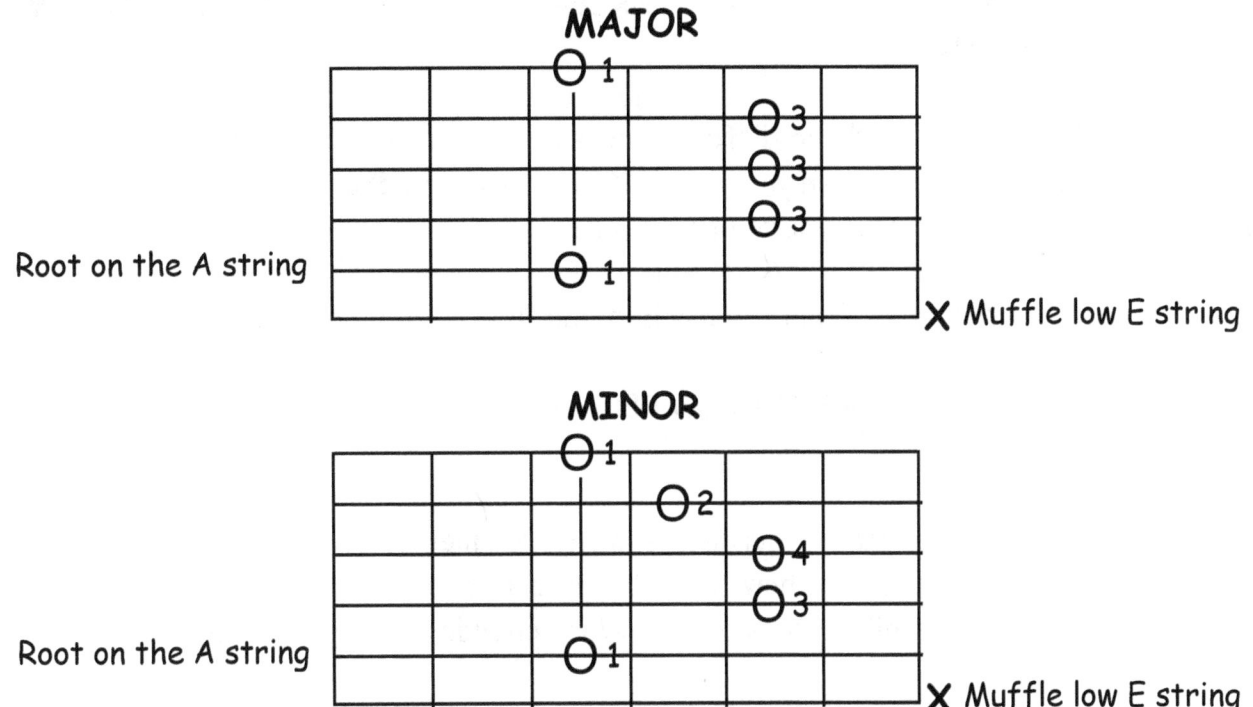

Once again, the numbers that you see on these diagrams represent each of your left hand fingers that are used to play these chords. And, yes, the 1st finger still has to "barre" across the neck of the guitar, this time clamping down on 5 strings in order to play these chords.

With these chord voicings, your 1st finger actually has to do double duty. Not only does it have to barre across the 5 strings, but also it has to poke up, ever so slightly, to just touch the low E string and muffle it. You don't want to press directly on the low E string, and you don't want to let it ring open when you strum these chords. So your 1st finger has to just rub up against it enough to muffle it completely. This will allow you to... do windmills with your right hand, dance about the stage, and sneer at audience members without worrying about having the low E string ring all the time.

This major voicing may elicit comments like, "No way!" or "There has to be a better way!". However, this is the fingering that you'll end up using, so you might as well start getting used to it now. Yes, your third finger has to kind of smoosh down and bend backwards in order to come up off the neck, down by the 1st string. It ain't pretty and it ain't easy, but after some time you will master it.

# I GOT YER QUESTIONS RIGHT HERE...

**IF ALL OF THESE BARRE CHORDS ARE "THREE-NOTE" CHORDS, HOW COME I'M PLAYING 5 OR 6 STRINGS?**

Good question.  There are only three different notes (letter names) that make up these 5 and 6 string barre chords.  So when you play a "G" major barre chord (with a root on the Low E string), the six notes that you're playing are:

G, D, G, B, D, G.

(these are the notes from the low E string "up" to the high E string)

**HOW DO ALL OF THESE BARRE CHORDS RELATE TO THE MAJOR SCALE?**

Another good question.
One of the biggest short-comings of guitarists is that we memorize the shapes of a bunch of chords, but we're not sure how they all relate to one another.  Why do some chords work well together, while others don't?  What chords do work well together?

Next I'll show how all of the barre chords fit into the major scale (you know, that scale that, at this point, you've learned thoroughly and grown to love completely and unconditionally).  Ideally, every time you play a chord, you should be able to see the scale that it belongs to, underneath your fingers on the neck of the guitar.

Once again, since we've been using the G major scale as a constant, we'll see how all of the barre chords fit into the G major scale.  And just to appease those who appreciate order, we'll start with the 1 chord on the low E string.  Remember that chords are built in 3rds, so the 1 chord is "spelled": 1 3 5.    The 2 chord is "spelled": 2 4 6   And so on...
G B D                                          A C E

Also remember that with triad harmony (three-note chords):
1, 4, and 5 chords = major chords     2, 3, and 6 chords = minor chords

AND the 7 chord is not a barre chord.

# ROOT ON LOW "E" STRING

Remember that with triad harmony (barre chords):
1, 4, and 5 chords = major chords      2, 3, and 6 chords = minor chords

## THE "1" BARRE CHORD IN "G" MAJOR

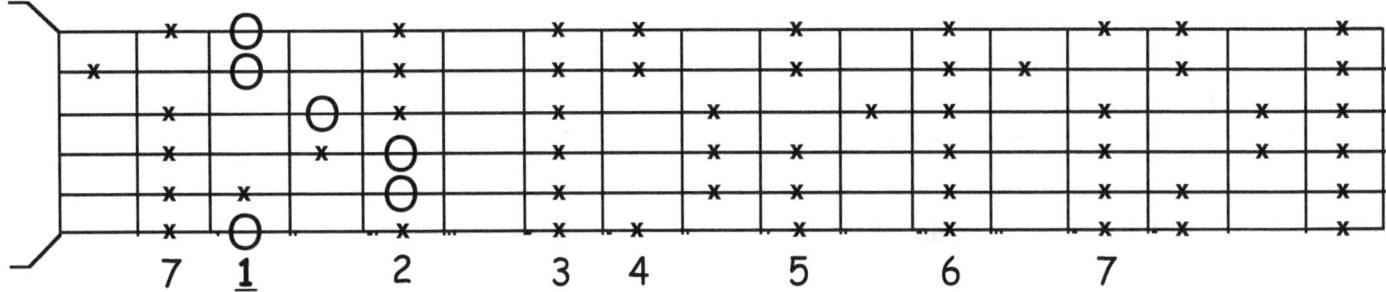

**Close up of "1" chord in pattern 7**

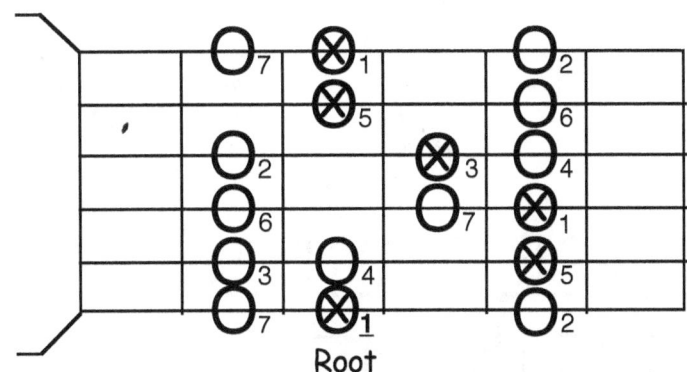

The 1 chord is spelled: 1, 3, 5.

Notice that even though you are playing all 6 strings, the only notes that you are actually playing are the 1, 3, and 5 of the G major scale.

More importantly, see how the major scale pattern lives underneath this 1 chord. The ability to "see" the major scale underneath every chord that you play, will enable you to embellish any chord and to solo freely at a moment's notice. It will also help when you are trying to compose a melody over any chord progression that you come up with.

For clarity, the "root" of every chord in these diagrams has been underlined.

Remember that with triad harmony (barre chords):
1, 4, and 5 chords = major chords     2, 3, and 6 chords = minor chords

# THE "2" BARRE CHORD IN "G" MAJOR

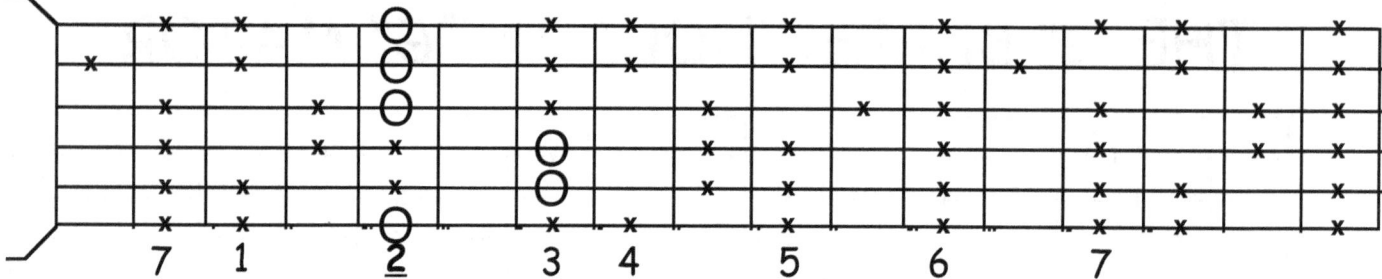

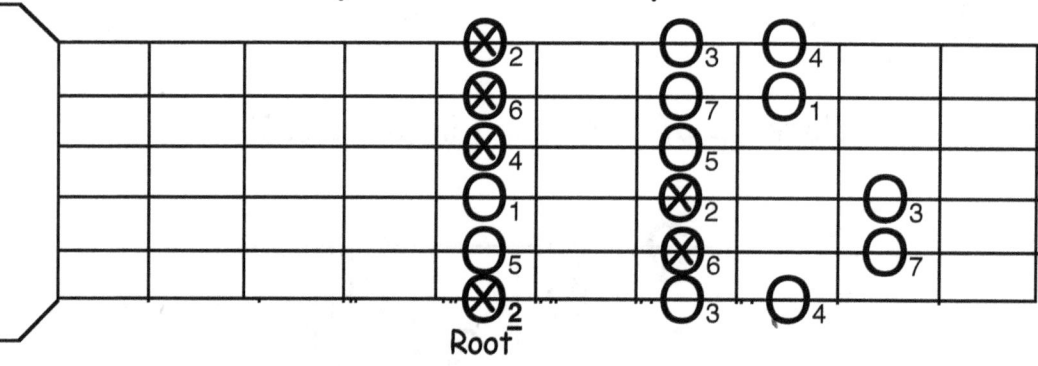

The 2 chord is spelled: 2, 4, 6.

# THE "3" BARRE CHORD IN "G" MAJOR

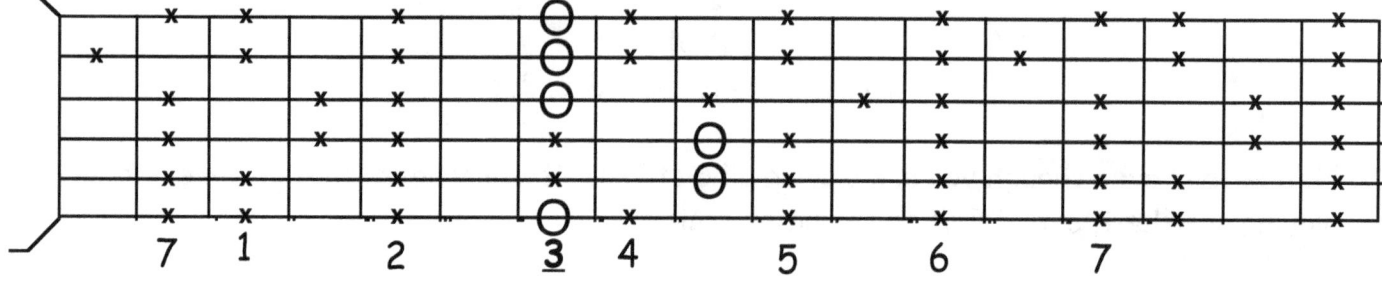

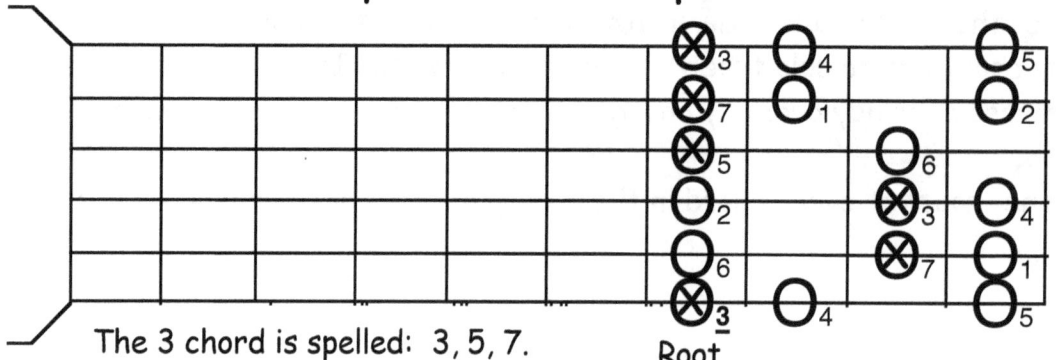

The 3 chord is spelled: 3, 5, 7.

Remember that with triad harmony (barre chords):
1, 4, and 5 chords = major chords    2, 3, and 6 chords = minor chords

# THE "4" BARRE CHORD IN "G" MAJOR

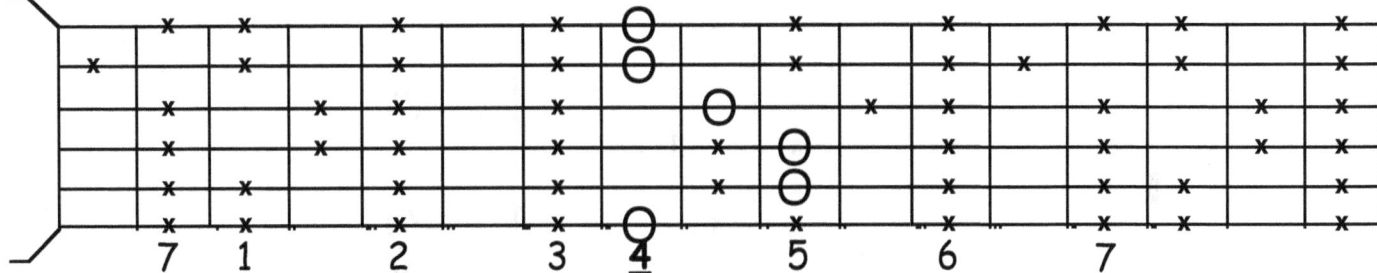

**Close up of "4" chord in pattern 3**

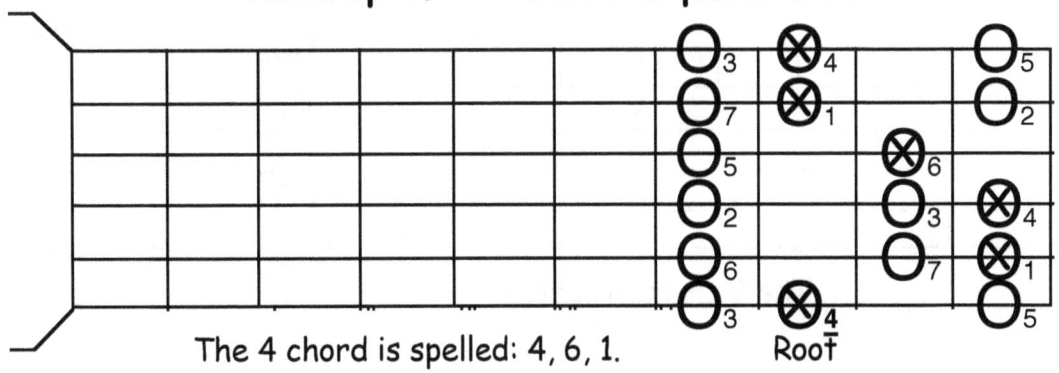

The 4 chord is spelled: 4, 6, 1.

# THE "5" BARRE CHORD IN "G" MAJOR

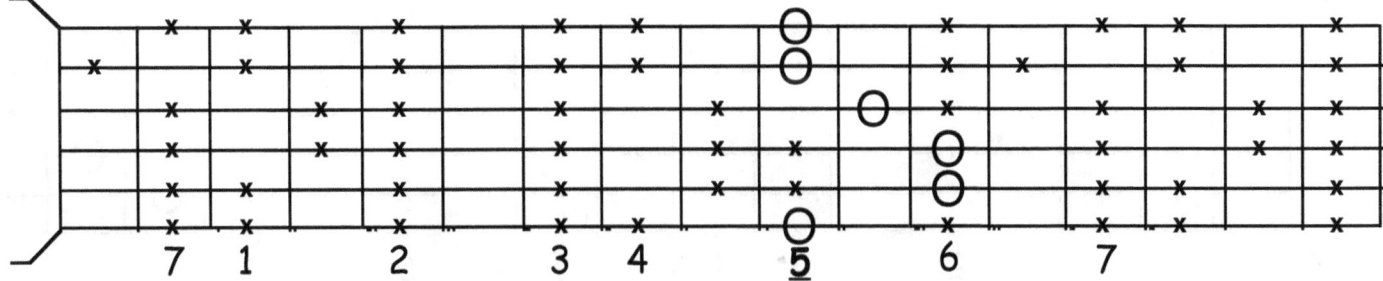

**Close up of "5" chord in pattern 4**

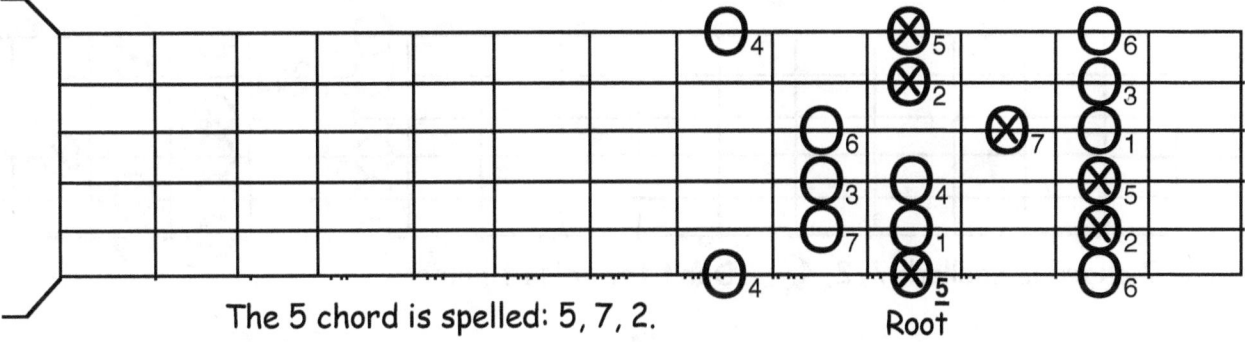

The 5 chord is spelled: 5, 7, 2.

Remember that with triad harmony (barre chords):
1, 4, and 5 chords = major chords    2, 3, and 6 chords = minor chords

# THE "6" BARRE CHORD IN "G" MAJOR

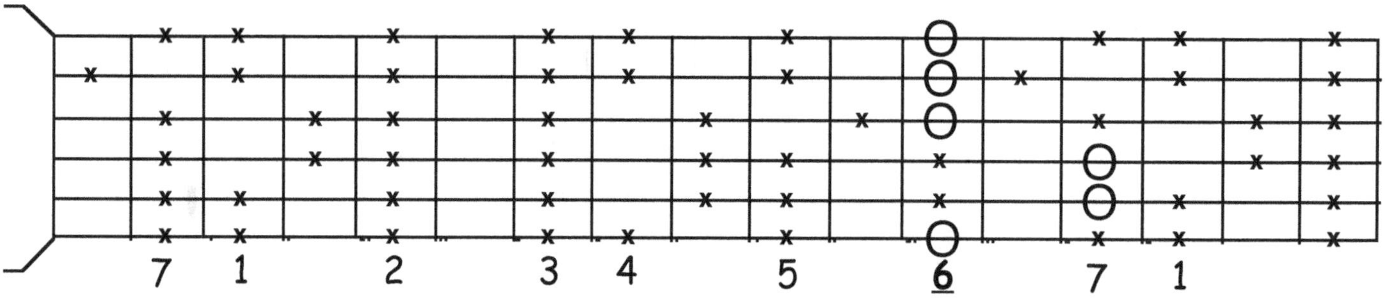

**Close up of "6" chord in pattern 6**

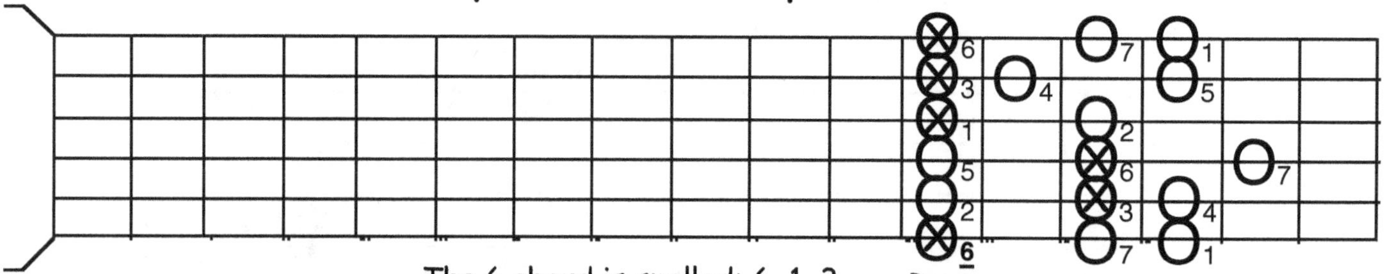

The 6 chord is spelled: 6, 1, 3.    Root

# THE "7" IS NOT A BARRE CHORD
(In fact, this is not a playable chord... what I'd give for a couple more fingers)

**Close up of what would be the "7" chord in pattern 6**

The 7 chord is spelled: 7, 2, 4.    Don't try this at home!

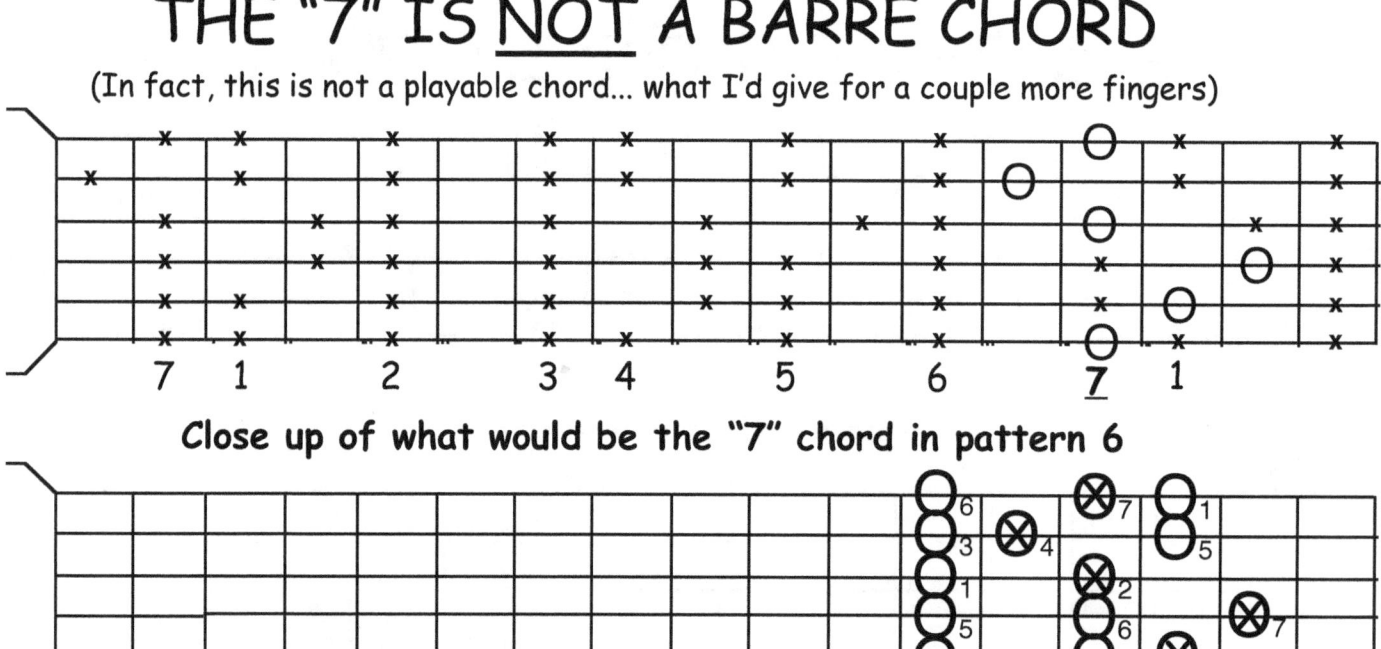

# ROOT ON THE "A" STRING

## THE "3" BARRE CHORD IN "G" MAJOR

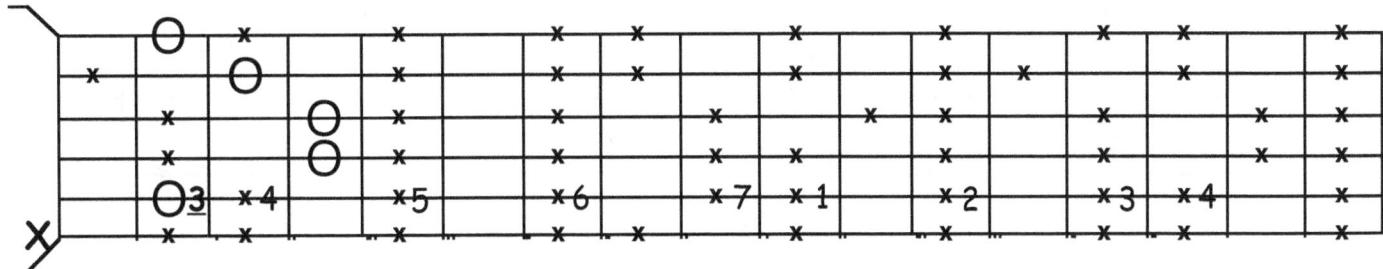

**Close up of "3" chord in pattern 7**

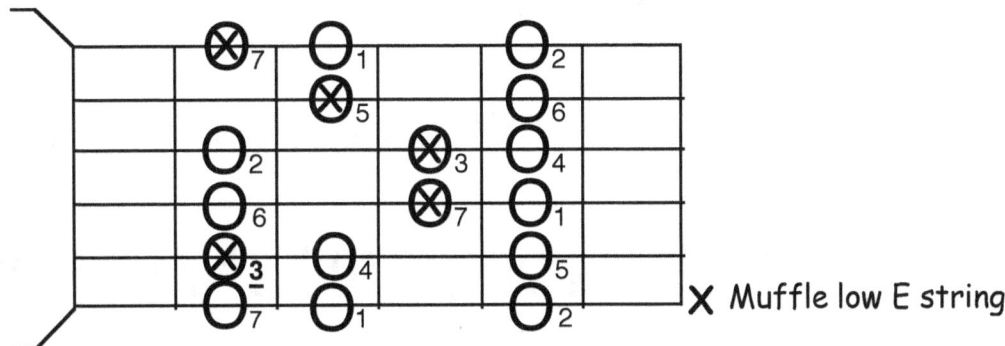

X Muffle low E string

The 3 chord is spelled: 3, 5, 7.

Now that these roots of the chords are on the A string, you'll have a whole new set of barre chords available under your fingers. You'll be able to play more than one chord within any one major scale pattern.

This means that getting to know the scale numbers for both the E string AND the A string are essential (barre chords can have their roots on either the E string OR the A string).

Remember that the "scale pattern number" comes from the note that your 1st finger starts with on the E string (not the A string).

Also remember that with triad harmony (barre chords):
1, 4, and 5 chords = major chords     2, 3, and 6 chords = minor chords

# THE "4" BARRE CHORD IN "G" MAJOR
## (Root on A string)

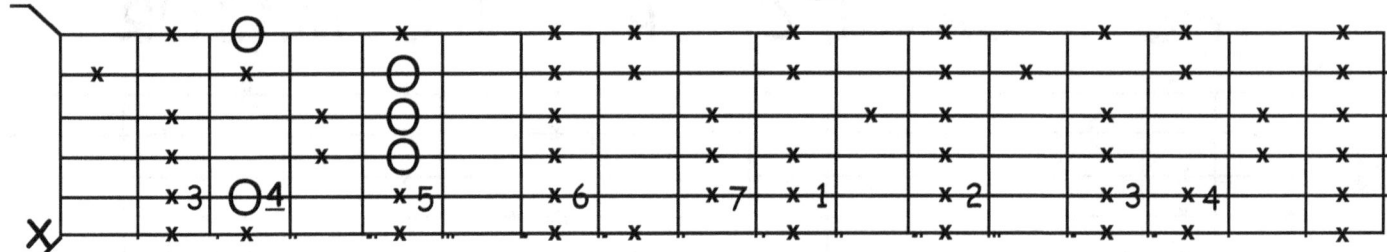

### Close up of "4" chord in pattern 7

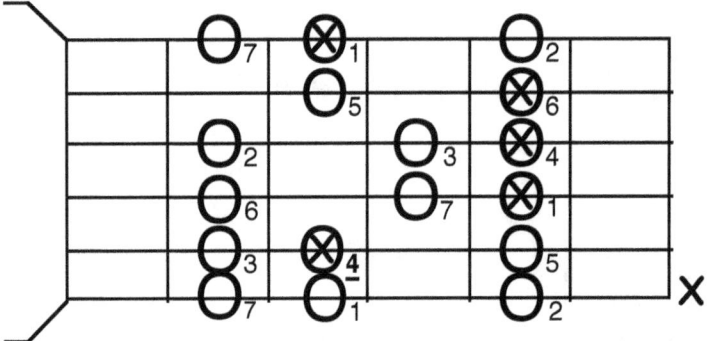

X Muffle low E string

The 4 chord is spelled: 4, 6, 1.

# THE "5" BARRE CHORD IN "G" MAJOR
## (Root on A string)

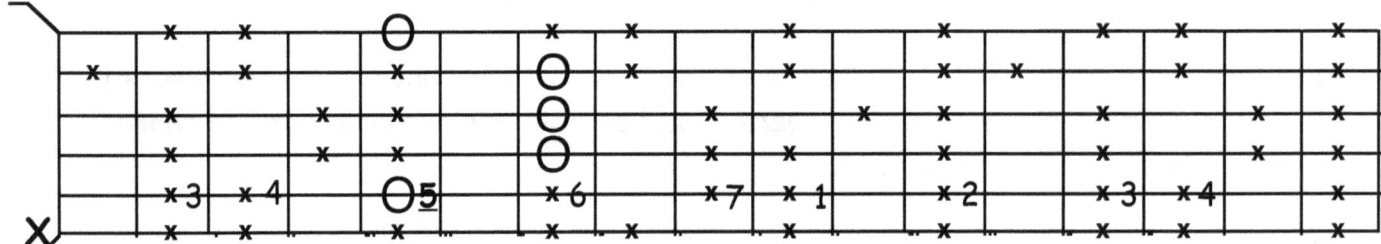

### Close up of "5" chord in pattern 2

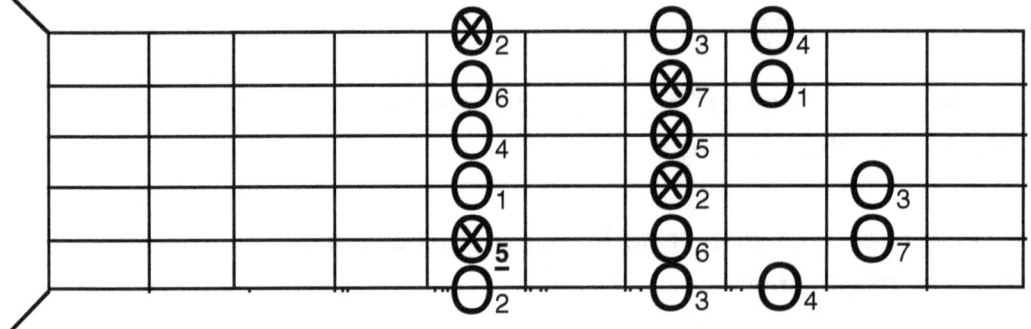

X Muffle low E string

The "5" chord is spelled: 5, 7, 2. And course, you remember that with triad harmony:
1, 4, & 5 chords = major chords and 2, 3, & 6 chords = minor chords.

45

# THE "6" BARRE CHORD IN "G" MAJOR
## (Root on A string)

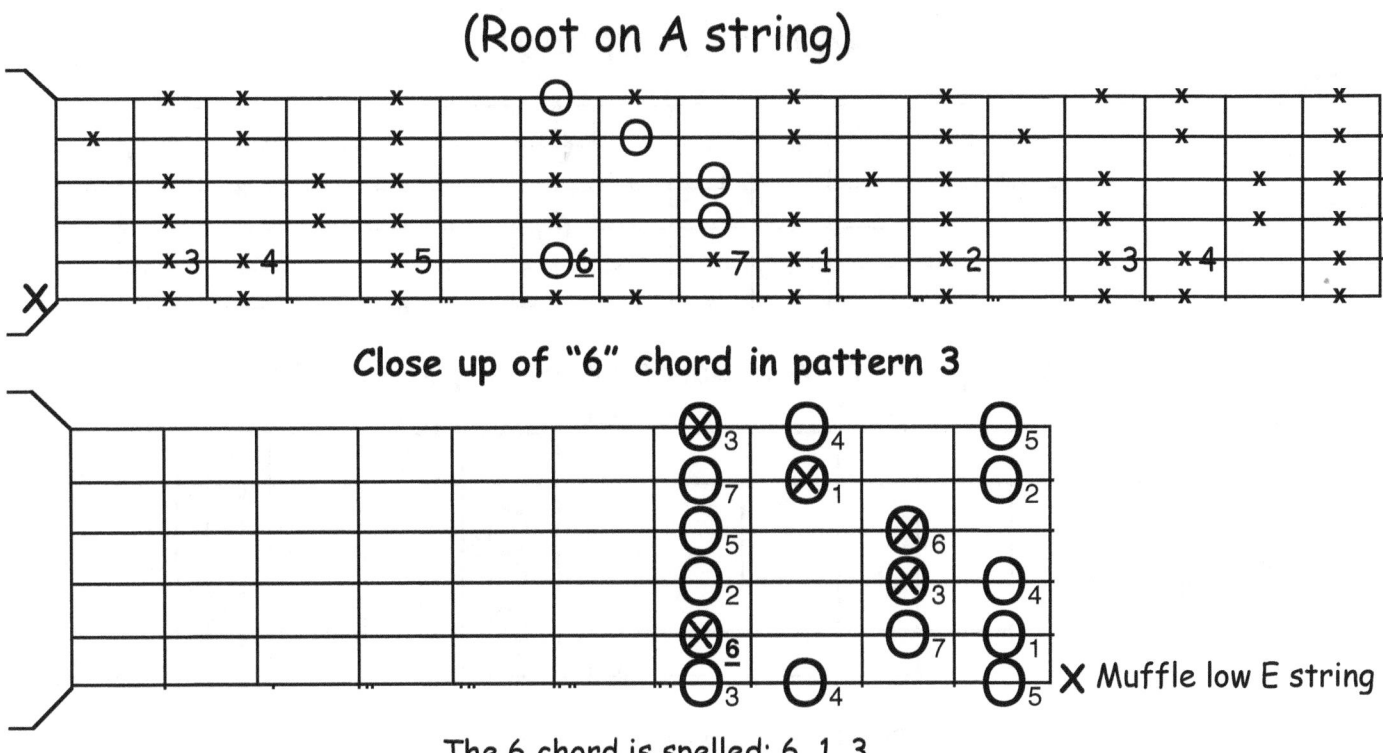

**Close up of "6" chord in pattern 3**

X Muffle low E string

The 6 chord is spelled: 6, 1, 3.

ALSO remember to muffle that low E string when you're playing these chords.
I've been reminding you on all of these "root on the A string barre chord" diagrams, but soon I'll run out of room on the right... so please remember.

AND, again, remember that with triad harmony (barre chords):
1, 4, and 5 chords = major chords     2, 3, and 6 chords = minor chords

# THE "7" NON-BARRE CHORD IN "G" MAJOR?!?

## (Root on A string)

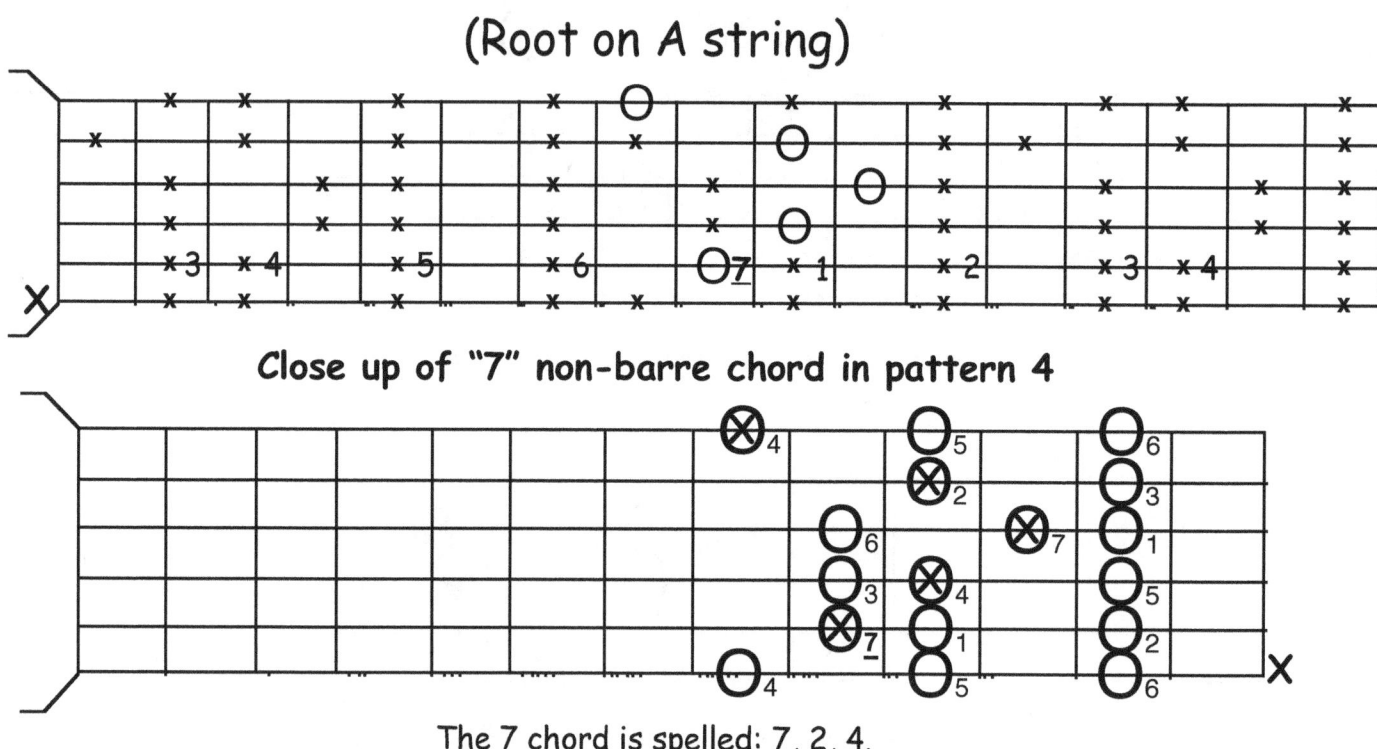

Close up of "7" non-barre chord in pattern 4

The 7 chord is spelled: 7, 2, 4.

Obviously we don't quite have enough fingers for this chord. You could probably figure out a way of playing it.... but why kill your hand? Remember that a 7 chord is spelled: 7, 2, 4. There are plenty of other cool options... like:

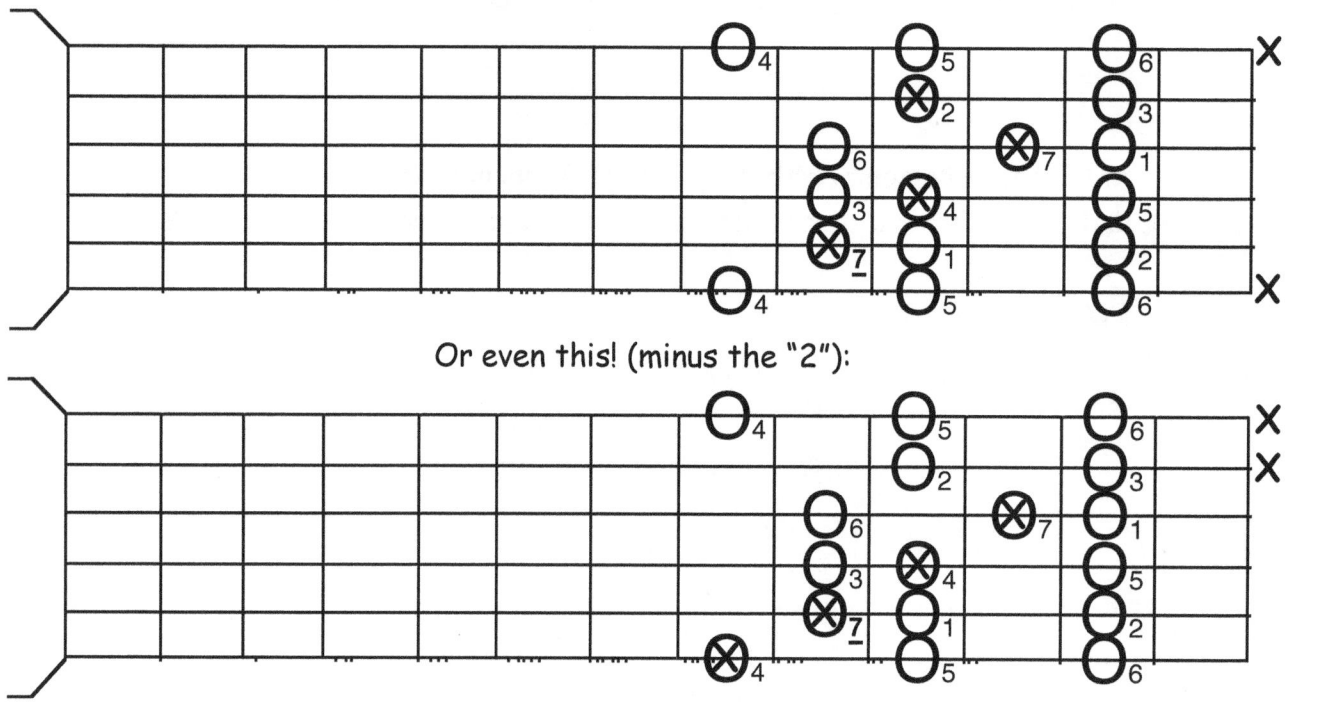

Or even this! (minus the "2"):

47

# THE "1" BARRE CHORD IN "G" MAJOR
## (Root on A string)

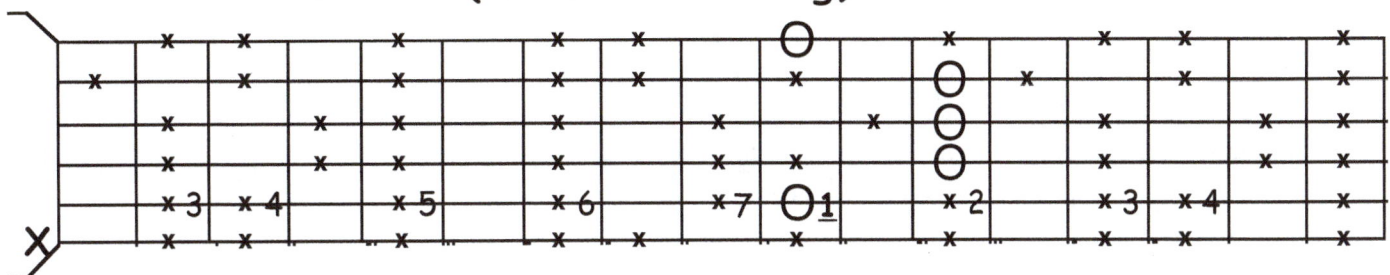

**Close up of "1" chord in pattern 4**

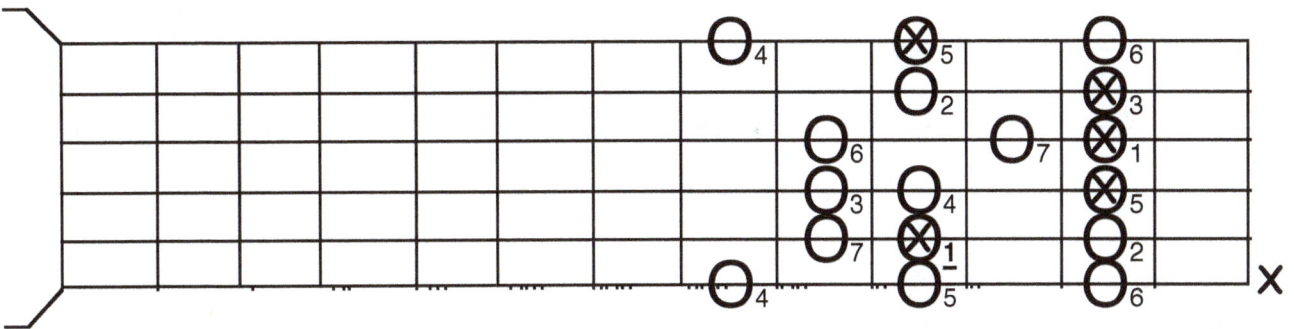

The 1 chord is spelled: 1, 3, 5.

You are remembering which barre chords are major and which are minor aren't you?
    (1, 4, and 5 chords = major chords    2, 3, and 6 chords = minor chords)

And you are, of course, muffling that pesky low E string when you're playing these "root on the A string" barre chords.... right?
..... just checking.

# THE "2" BARRE CHORD IN "G" MAJOR
## (Root on A string)

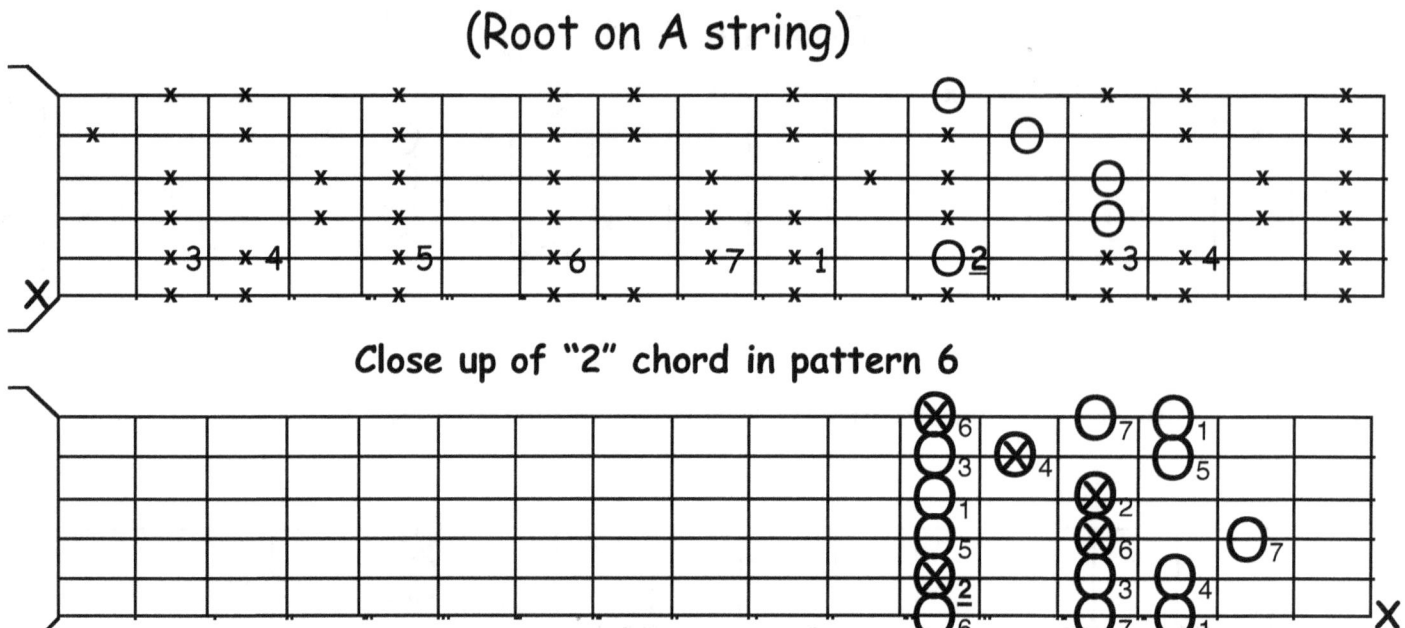

**Close up of "2" chord in pattern 6**

The 2 chord is spelled: 2, 4, 6.

Hmmmm, no reminders on this page?

Could this be right?

By this time, do you actually know what the tonalities are for the barre chords of a major scale?

Can I ask any more annoying questions?

Should I stop this tired routine?

...Now?

...How about now?

# E & A STRING ROOT RELATIONSHIPS

Because the barre chords only have roots on the E string and the A string, you will have to know the major scale numbers (where the roots are) on both strings AND see how they relate to each other. If you were in the key of G major, this is where all of the barre chords would be located.

When you change keys, all of these numbers will shift up or down on the neck BUT they will stay in the same order and they'll still have this exact same spacing relationship to each other.

ALSO these are exactly the same shapes and order for the upcoming 4 note chord root relationships. So this is pretty important to know!

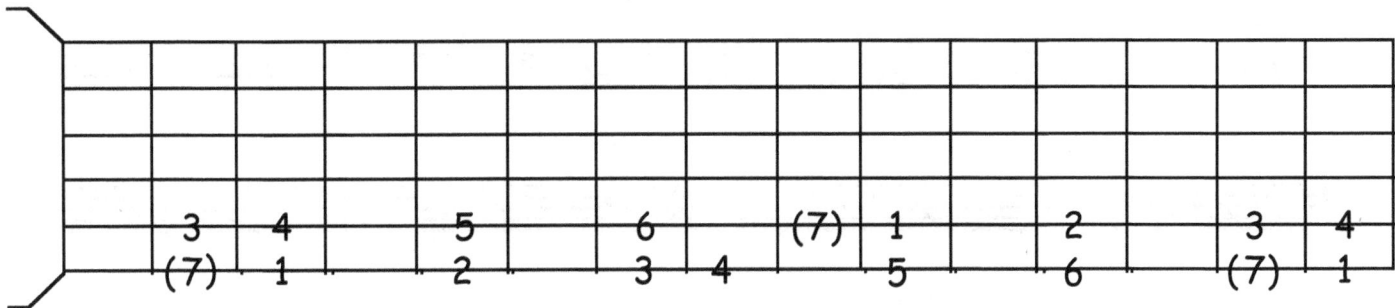

You will also need to know where all of the notes are on the E string and the A string...
...remember?

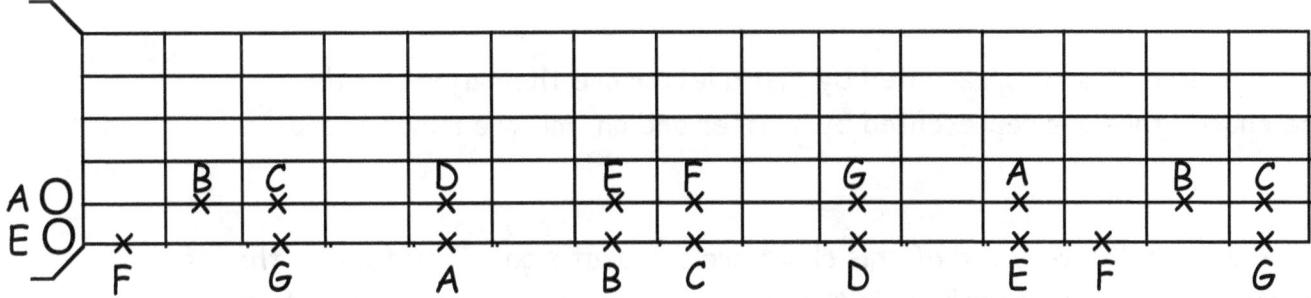

Now that you're getting the hang of the barre chords... (I know that some of you are still thinking that there is no way in Heck that you're ever going to be comfortable with barre chords... you will), let's try to see if we can start using them. I have written out a sample chord chart for us to use. The chords here are all related.

Your mission will be to:

1) Play this chart. Remember, you've got two different choices of where to play each of these chords ("root on the low E" barre chord OR "root on the A" barre chord)

2) Figure out how these chords are related. We'll talk about this more later.

## CHORD CHART EXAMPLE 1

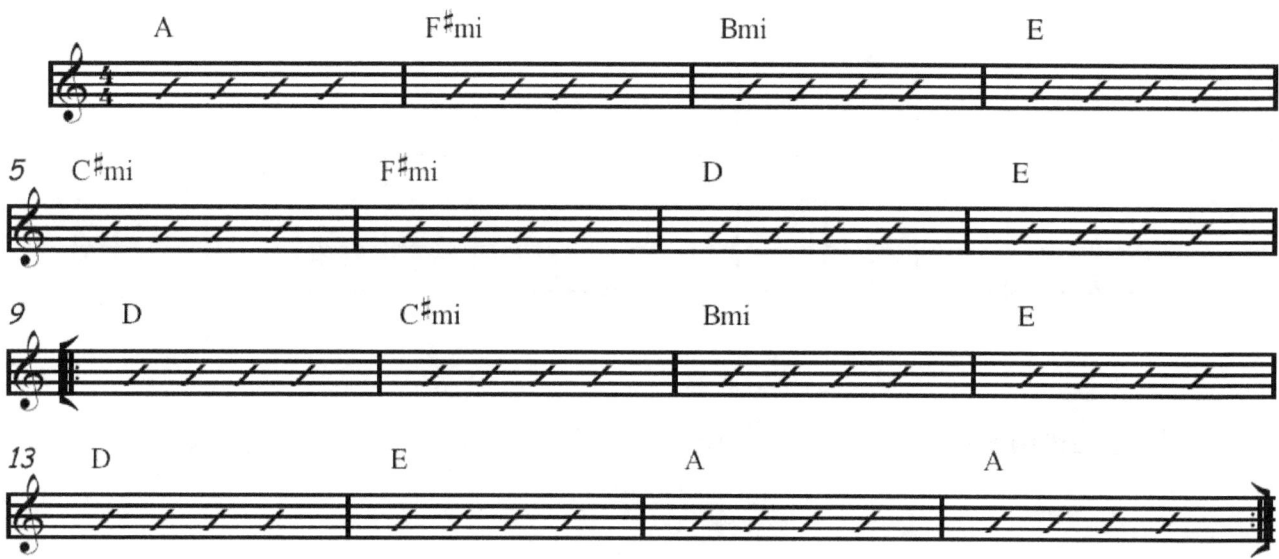

The chords that are represented by just a letter are the major chords.
The chords that are represented by a letter and an "mi" are minor chords.

The 2 dots at the very end of this chart are a repeat sign. They face to the left, indicating that you repeat back in the chart. You must look for the 2 dots that you passed that were facing to the right and repeat back to this point in the chart. If there were no other dots on the chart, you would have to go back to the top and play the whole chart again. When reading any chart, ALWAYS look for the road maps BEFORE you launch into playing it, or you'll get lost every time. Each one of the slash-type notes in each measure represent a strum on the guitar. Notice that there are 4 strums in each measure.

When you are first analyzing a chord chart, you need to see if all or most of the chords that you're given share a common key. In "Chord Chart Example 1", you've got the following chords: A, F#min, Bmin, E, C#min, D.

At this point, you know that with triad harmony (barre chords):
1, 4, and 5 chords = major chords      2, 3, and 6 chords = minor chords

This means that the A, D, & E chords are either 1's, 4's, or 5 chords.
And the F#min, Bmin, & C#min chords are either 2's, 3's, or 6 chords.

Since the example starts with an A major chord, lets first look at the major chords. You will need to know the letter names on the A and E strings (but of course you know these by now). Once you find the A on the low E string, you can see that the D lives right underneath it, and the E is just up 2 frets from the D.

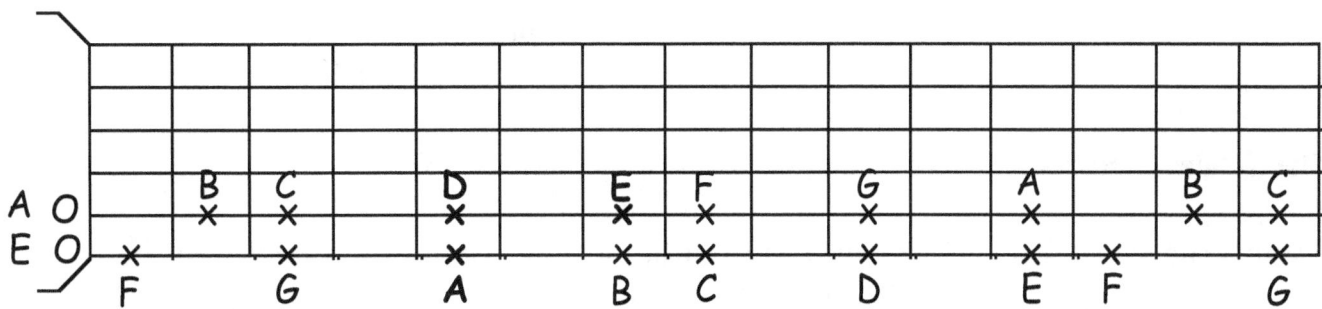

This pattern is a common pattern AND if you recall the "root relationships" within a major scale (see below), you'll notice that the A, D, and E pattern fits nicely into a 1, 4, 5 pattern.

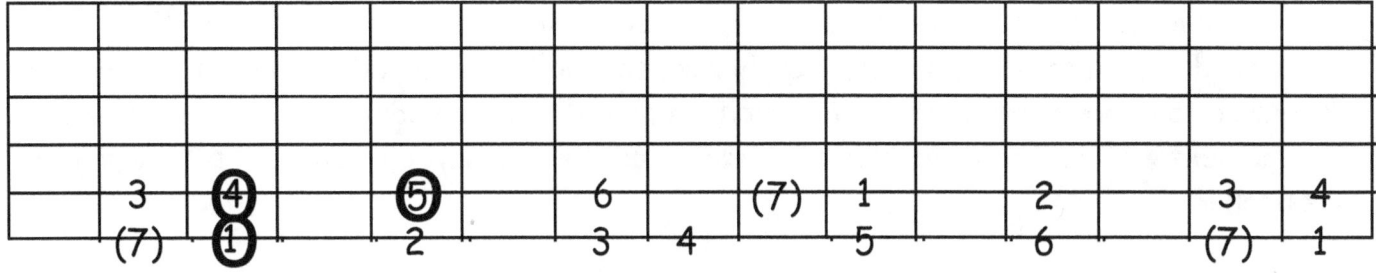

Since the name of the major scale comes from whatever the 1 is, it looks like these three chords fit into the key of A major. If you try to fit the minor chords into the key of A major, you'll see that the "B"min chord is the 2 chord (up 2 frets from the 1 chord). The "C#"min chord fits as the 3 chord (up 4 frets from the 1 chord...remember that a sharp is 1 fret up from the letter name). And the "F#"min chord fits as the 6 chord (remember that the 6 chord is always up 2 frets from the 5 chord or down 3 frets from the 1 chord).

# FOUR-NOTE CHORDS

Remember that each of the 7 notes of the major scale can have a chord built on it. And each of these 7 chords that come from the major scale have a sound or a "tonality". The words that are used to describe these tonalities are as follows:

| TRIAD TONALITY | SEVENTH TONALITY |
| --- | --- |
| 1 Chord= Major | 1 Chord= Major 7 |
| 2 Chord= Minor | 2 Chord= Minor 7 |
| 3 Chord= Minor | 3 Chord= Minor 7 |
| 4 Chord= Major | 4 Chord= Major 7 |
| 5 Chord= Major | 5 Chord= Dominant 7 |
| 6 Chord= Minor | 6 Chord= Minor 7 |
| 7 Chord= Minor b5 or Diminished | 7 Chord= Minor 7 b5 or Half Diminished |

**(The following history is to be served with a large helping of salt)**

Seventh chords are used all over in today's music. In the 30's and 40's (and even the 50's) seventh chords were used in most, if not all, of the popular music. These chords have a rich, full sound to them. As Rock & Roll began to "evolve", players started wanting a more primal sound, something with less color and with more raw energy. This is what prompted the removal of the 7th from the basic chord and lead to the wide use of barre chords in the 50's, 60's, and 70's. And if raw is cool, than "rawer" must be cooler! So in the 80's and 90's the barre chord was stripped of its 3rd and only the roots and 5ths were used. This provides for a completely raw, bare jolt of stripped down harmony that has more to do with the rhythm with which it's played than the color which it provides. Maybe next we'll just play one note at a time... and then .... maybe no notes.... silence will be back in style!

...maybe not.

When dealing with 7th chords (4 note chords), **YOU WILL HAVE TO KNOW** the "tonality" of each of the 7 possible chords (THIS IS IMPORTANT):

>1 & 4 chords = Major 7
>2, 3, & 6 chords = Minor 7
>5 chord = Dominant 7
>7 chord = Minor 7b5 (or half diminished)

At this point we're not going to get into the math of why a 4 chord is a major 7 chord and a 5 chord in a dominant 7 chord or what these names mean (I'll leave that to the many books and teachers that are already out there).

What you need to know is:
1) What do these chords look like on a chord chart?
2) What do these chords look like on the neck of the guitar?

Unfortunately, there is no standard notation for writing out chord symbols on chord charts. There are, however, some symbols that are used more frequently then others. I'll use the letter C as a constant to show you these symbols:

>C Major 7 = C Maj7, C M7, C Major7, C △7, C Ma7
>
>C Minor 7 = C-7, C min7, C m7, C mi7
>
>C Dominant 7 = C7 (This symbol is pretty universal)
>
>C Minor 7b5 = C-7b5, Cø7, Cmin7b5, C mi7b5

So the symbols are recognizable and pretty self-explanatory. Your job will be to remember what they look like AND remember:

>1 & 4 chords = Major 7
>2, 3, & 6 chords = Minor 7
>5 chord = Dominant 7
>7 chord = Minor 7b5

...And, of course, you'll have to learn the shapes and fingerings for each of these chord types. There are many places on the guitar to play each of these chord types. We'll learn 3 different places to play each chord (this will be a good chunk of information and it will give you a decent starting chord vocabulary).

Each of these three sets of chord voicings will use a different set of strings (string groupings):

1) Root on the low E string (Split over the A string).  These are chords that primarily use the low strings.

2) Root on the A string (Inside 4 strings).  These are chords that use the middle strings.

3) Root on the D string (Top 4 strings).  These are chords that use the high strings.

# "Root On The Low E String"
## (Split over the A string)

With this 1st set of chord voicings, you will have to muffle the A string and the high E string.  To muffle the A string, your 1st finger will have to lean down a bit, in order to just touch the A string so as not to let it ring.  This is good for all of these voicings except the 7 chord.  With this voicing, you'll have to use your 2nd finger to lean down and muffle the A string.

In order to muffle the high E string, just use whichever finger is on the B string (the closest to the high E string) and lean down a bit to keep the high E string from ringing.  This way you can strum the chord and not be too worried about hitting any unwanted strings.  This will take a little practice and will feel a bit awkward at first, but its not that difficult and before you know it, you'll start doing it automatically.

All of this will make SOOOO much more sense when you see the actual fingerings for these chords.  So.....

# "ROOT ON THE LOW E STRING" CHORD VOICINGS

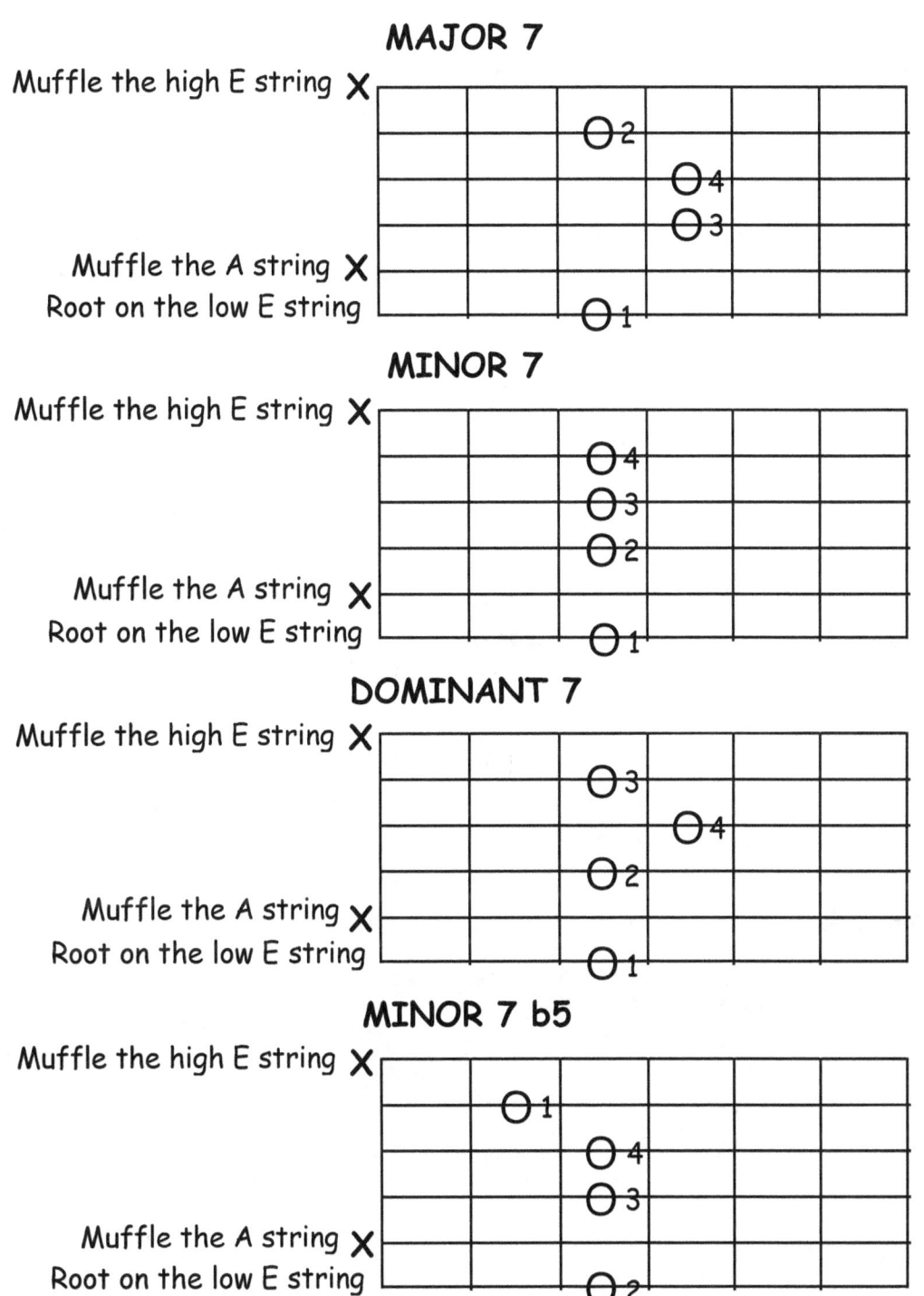

The numbers in these diagrams represent each of the left hand fingers you should use. Also, remember to muffle that high E string as well.

# "Root On The A String"
## (Inside 4 strings)

This set of chord voicings is an awful lot like the barre chords with the root on the A string. Your 1st finger will have to barre down across all 5 strings (muffling the low E string) for all of these voicings except the 7 chord (minor7b5).

The note that the lower part of your 1st finger plays on the high E string (when barring across the neck) is a doubling of the note that your 3rd finger plays. The only difference between these notes is that the note that your 1st finger is on is one octave up from the note that your 3rd finger is on.

Joe Pass (an amazing guitarist who no longer walks amongst us) might take issue with this doublng of a note. He was pretty particular about his voicings. His thinking was that since we only have the four fingers of our left hand to form chords, and since 7th chords have four notes in them (not counting extensions or alterations), if we were going to double any note of a chord, it had to be for a VERY good reason. I learned this the hard way, when during a lesson with him, he stopped me in the middle of a tune and asked if I really intended to double the note that I was doubling, and if so why....
... one could only imagine what he would have to say about barre chords!!

HOWEVER, at this point we need to build up our chord vocabulary, so don't worry about doubling a note here or there. The objective here is to increase our knowledge of 7th voicings and these voicings are used all over the place in music today.

Remember to muffle that low E string with the tip of your first finger.

Here are the "Root on the A String" voicings:

# "ROOT ON THE A STRING" CHORD VOICINGS

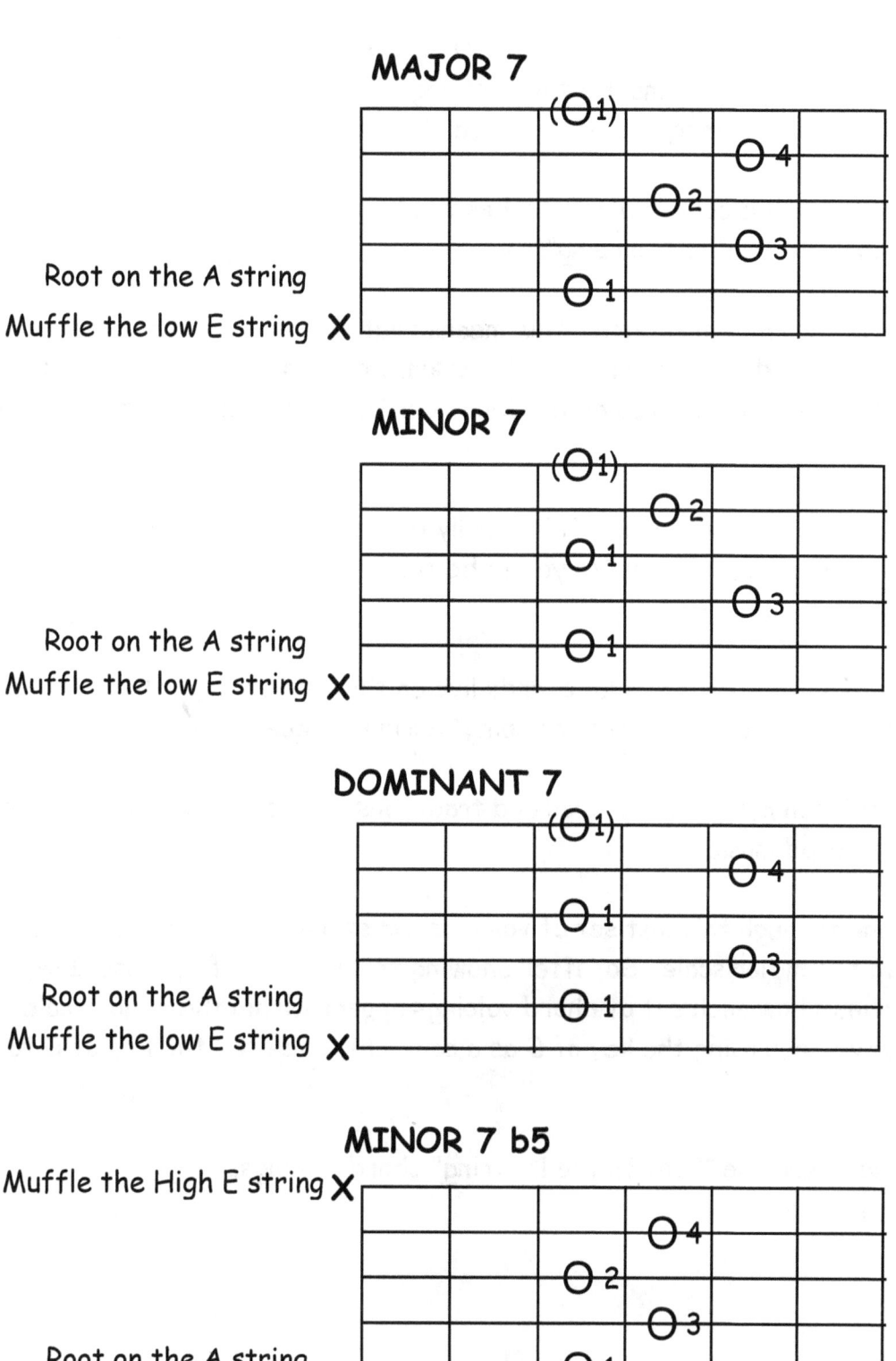

# "Root On The D String"
## (Top 4 strings)

This set of chord voicings doesn't use the A string or the low E string. Your first finger can poke up ever so slightly to muffle the A string. As for the low E string, just make sure that you don't hit it when you strum these chords.

For guitar, there are basically two approaches to playing chords during a song. You will either be playing "Rhythm" or "Comping".

"Rhythm" stands for rhythm section. This means that the chords that you play need to be harmonically full and rhythmically steady. Usually one would use the "Root On The Low E (Split over the A string)" chords or the "Root On The A (Inside 4 string)" chords for this function.

"Comping" stands for accompanying. This usually means that the rhythm function is being covered by someone else and its up to you to be freer with your rhythms; jabbing and poking about with the harmony.

Because these "Root on the D string" chords live on the high strings, these chords are more frequently played when you are "comping" during a piece of music.

As with everything in music, these rules and traditions can be ignored or broken as long as you can make good music.

Once we've gone through this last set of voicings, we still need to "see" how these 7th chords fit into the major scale. So, after showing this last set of voicings, I've included a section that shows how each set of chord voicings appear within the major scale. And again, since we've been using the key of G as a constant, I've used the key of G to do this.

Here, at long last, are the "Root on the D string" chord voicings...

# "ROOT ON THE D STRING" CHORD VOICINGS

### MAJOR 7

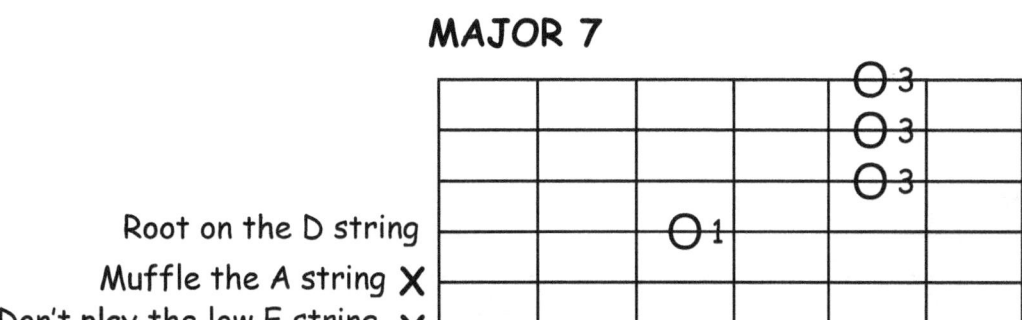

### MINOR 7

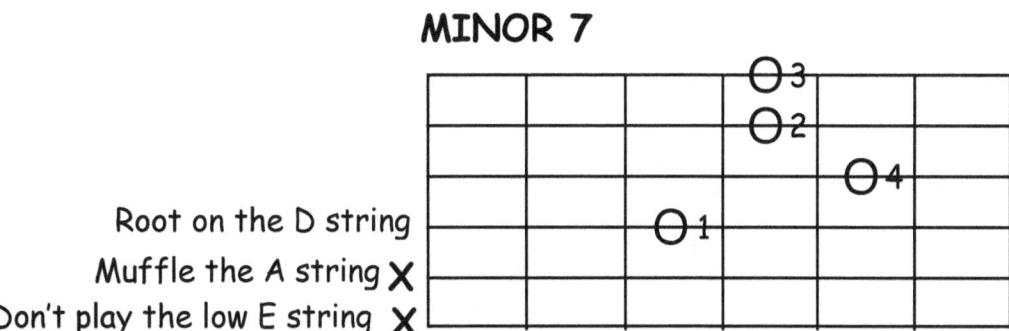

### DOMINANT 7

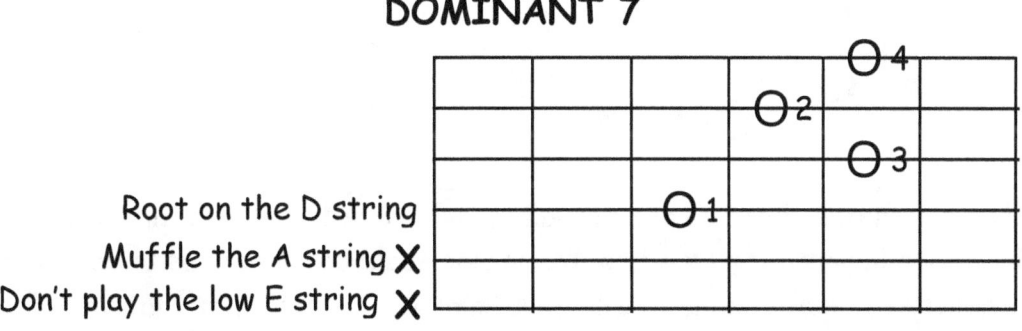

### MINOR 7 b5

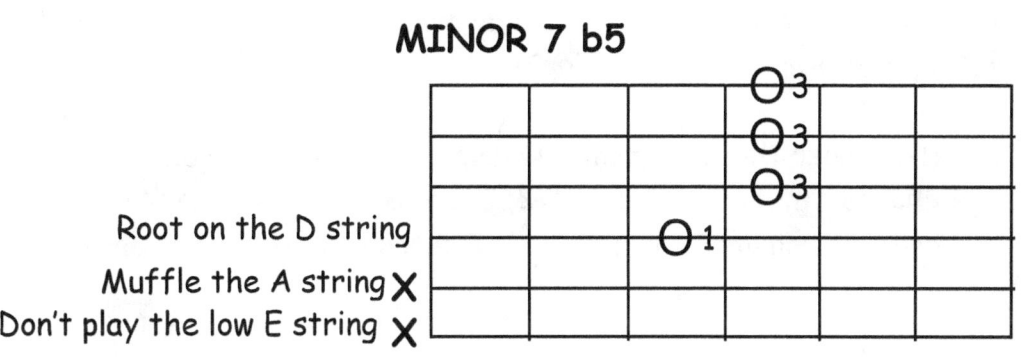

# ROOT ON THE "E" STRING
## (Split Over The "A" String)

## THE "1" SEVENTH CHORD IN "G" MAJOR

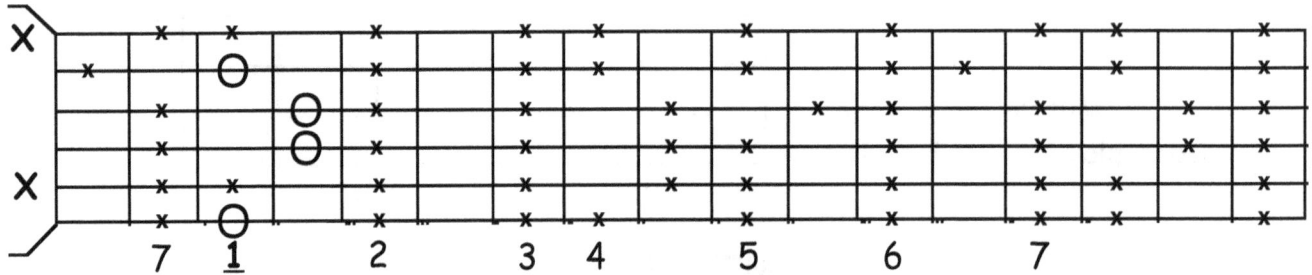

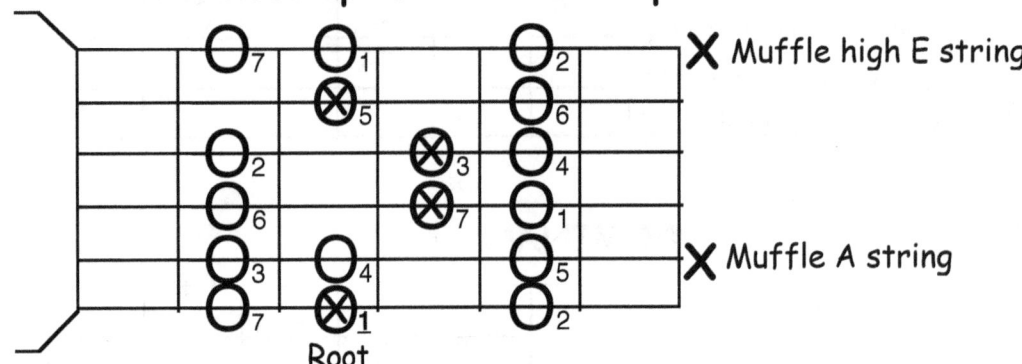

Notice that the only notes that you are actually playing are the 1, 3, 5, and 7 of the G major scale. More importantly, see how the major scale pattern lives underneath this 1 chord. The ability to "see" the major scale underneath every chord that you play, will enable you to embellish any chord and to solo freely at a moment's notice. It will also help when you are trying to come up with a melody over any chord progression that you compose. (Does this paragraph sound familiar?)

Remember that with quartal harmony (seventh chords):
1 and 4 chords = major7 chords    2, 3, and 6 chords = minor7 chords
5 chords = dominant7 chords    7 chords = minor7b5 chords

# THE "2" SEVENTH CHORD IN "G" MAJOR
## (Root on the low E String)

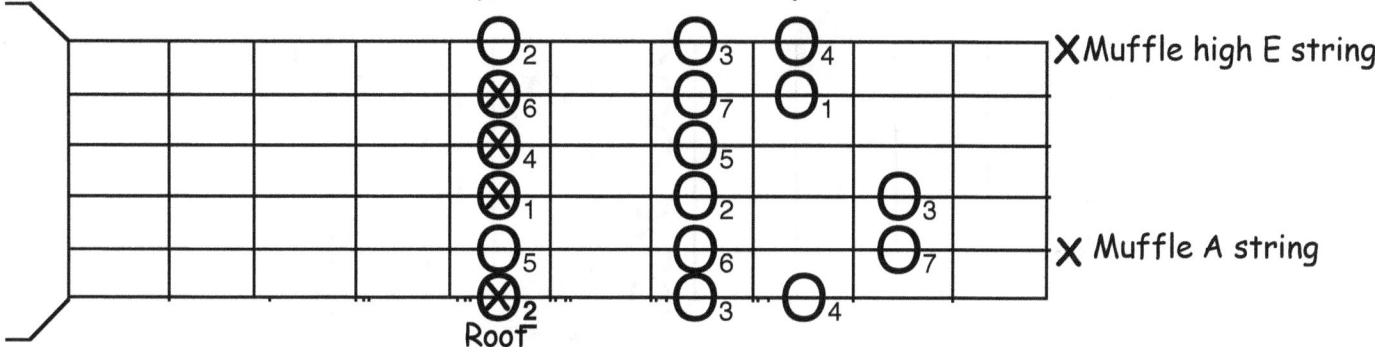

### Close up of "2" chord in pattern 2

Notice that the only notes that you are playing are the 2, 4, 6, and 1 of the G major scale.

# THE "3" SEVENTH CHORD IN "G" MAJOR
## (Root on the low E string)

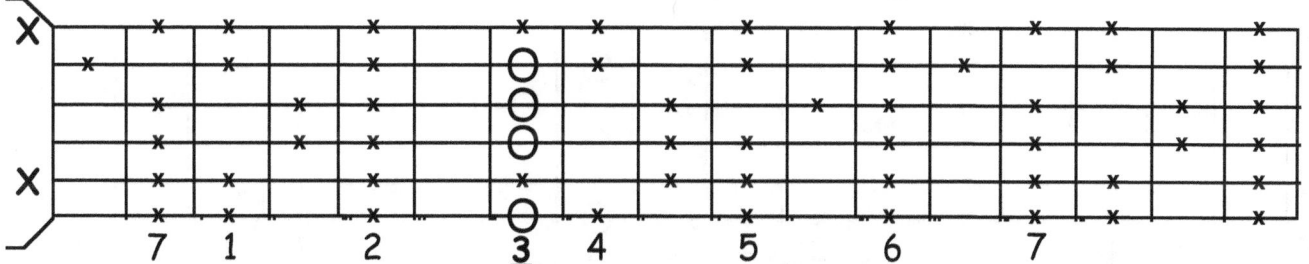

### Close up of "3" chord in pattern 3

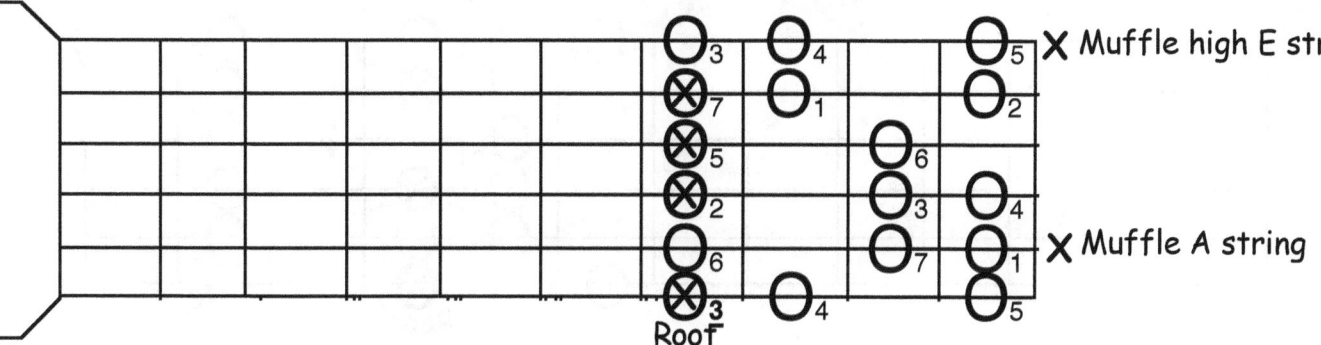

The 3 chord is spelled: 3, 5, 7, 2. Do you remember the tonalities of the seventh chords?

# THE "4" SEVENTH CHORD IN "G" MAJOR
## (Root on the low E string)

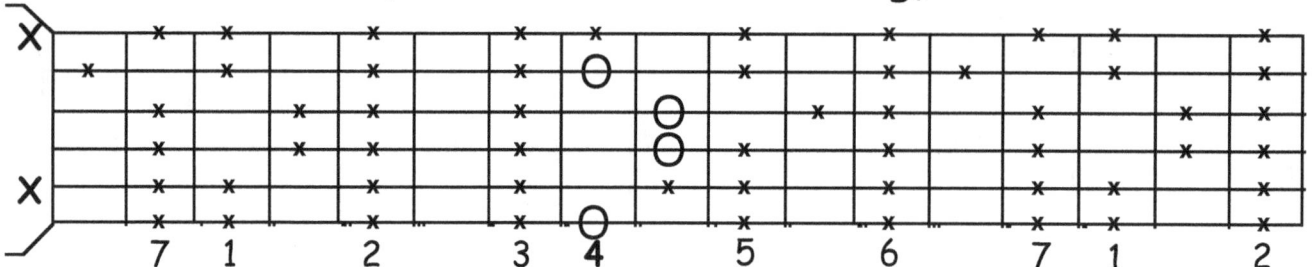

### Close up of "4" chord in pattern 3

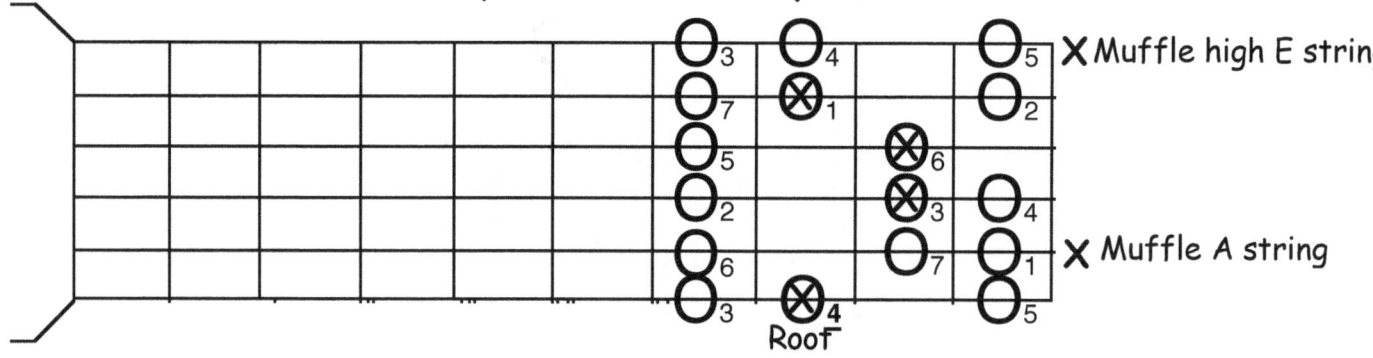

The 4 chord is spelled: 4, 6, 1, 3.

# THE "5" SEVENTH CHORD IN "G" MAJOR
## (Root on the low E string)

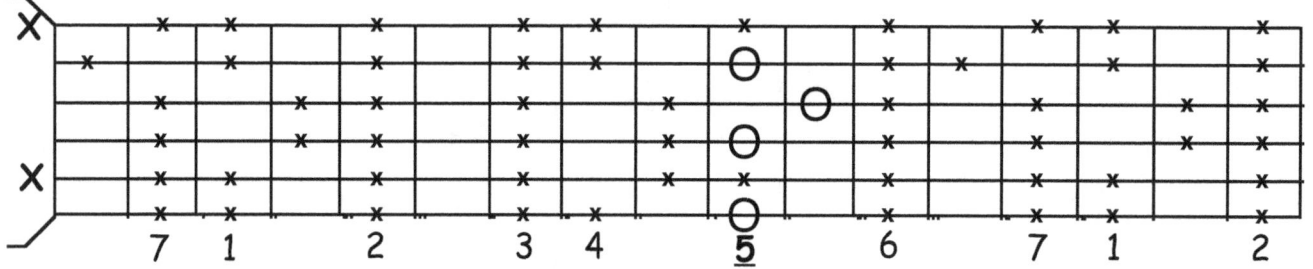

### Close up of "5" chord in pattern 4

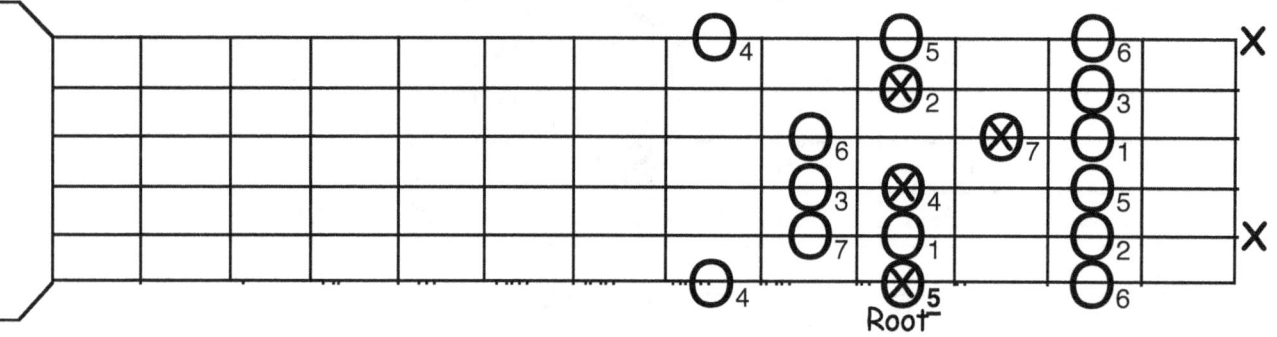

The 5 chord is spelled: 5, 7, 2, 4

And, of course, you still remember the tonalities of the seventh chords... right?

# THE "6" SEVENTH CHORD IN "G" MAJOR
## (Root on the low E string)

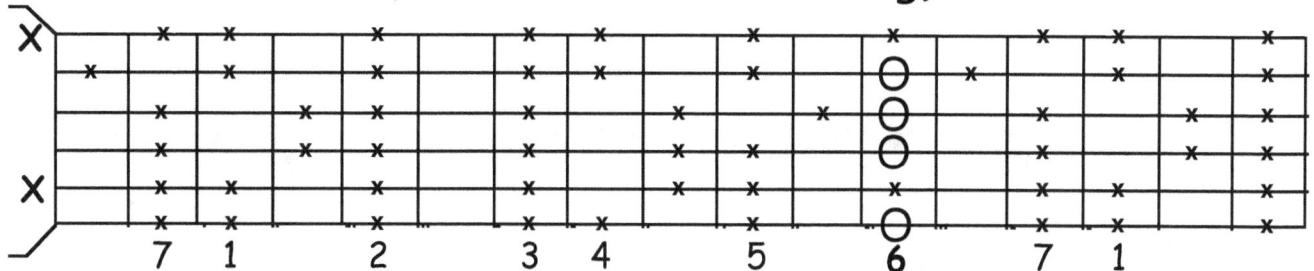

**Close up of "6" chord in pattern 6**

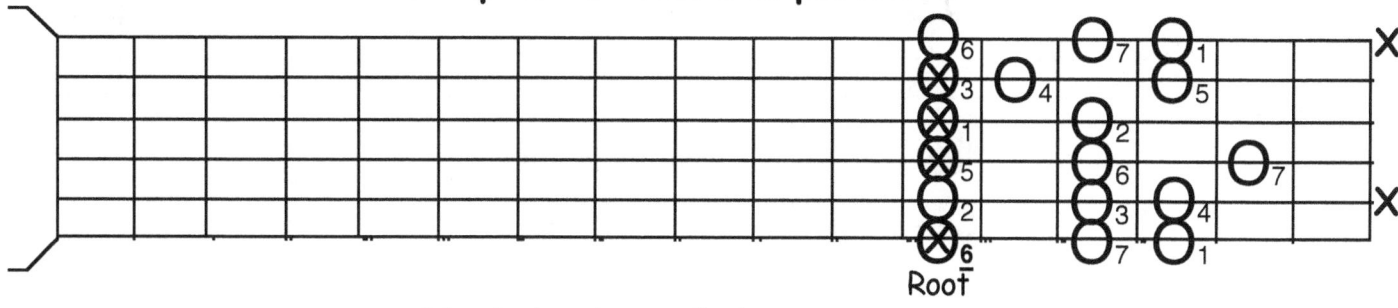

The 6 chord is spelled: 6, 1, 3, 5.

# THE "7" SEVENTH CHORD IN "G" MAJOR
## (Root on the low E string)

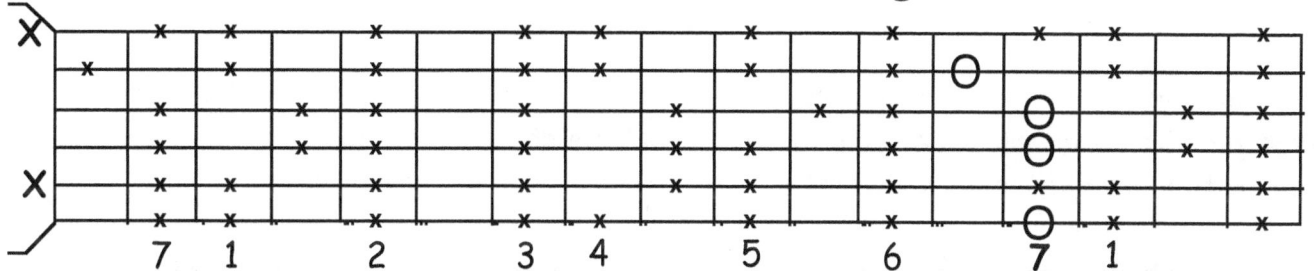

**Close up of the "7" chord in pattern 6**

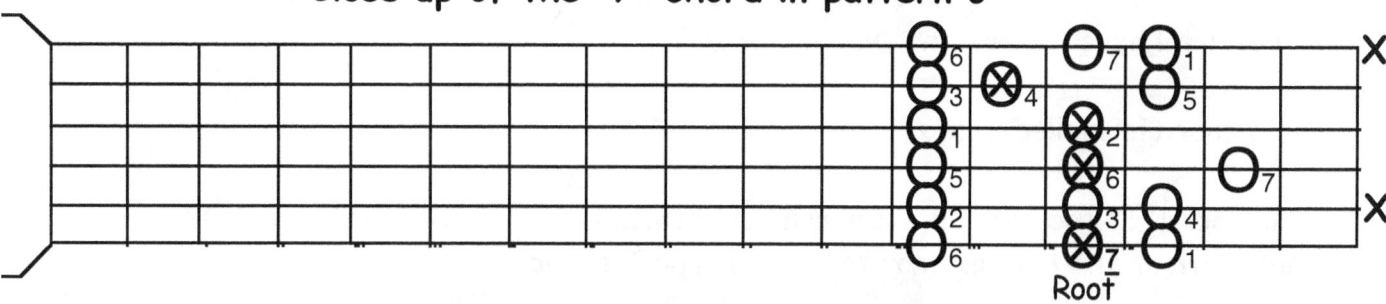

The 7 chord is spelled: 7, 2, 4, 6...   Tonality, schmonality ... but remember:
1 and 4 chords = major7 chords    2, 3, and 6 chords = minor7 chords
5 chords = dominant7 chords       7 chords = minor7b5 chords

# ROOT ON THE "A" STRING
## (Inside 4 Strings)

## THE "3" SEVENTH CHORD IN "G" MAJOR

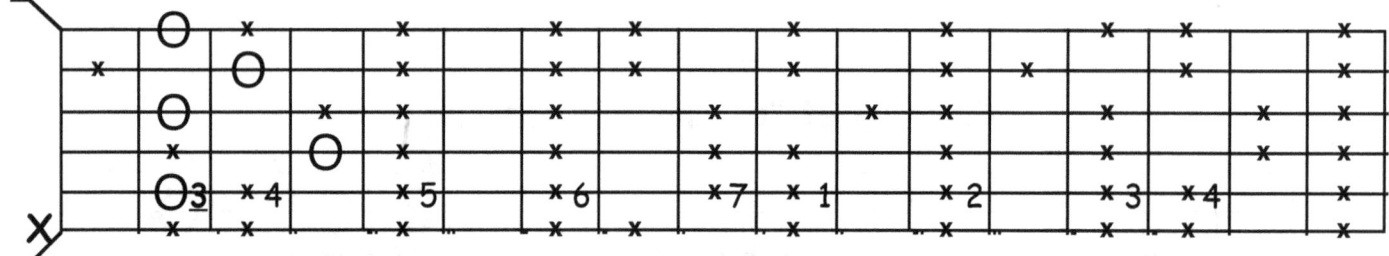

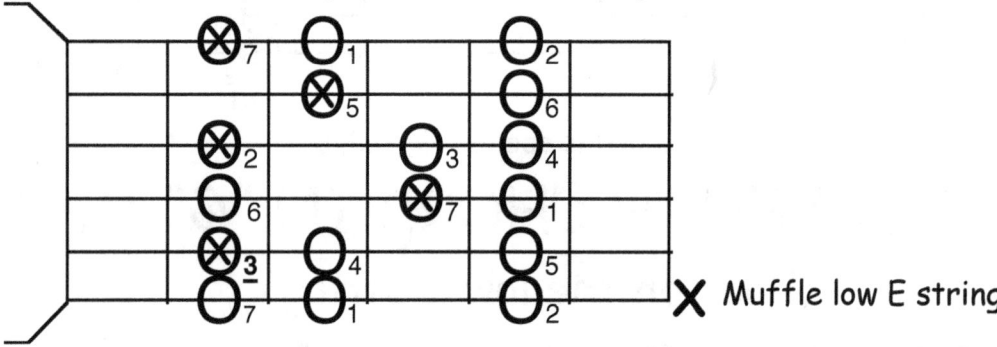

Close up of "3" chord in pattern 7

X Muffle low E string

Now that the roots of the chords are on the A string, you'll have a whole new set of seventh chords available under your fingers. You'll be able to play more than one seventh chord within any one major scale pattern.

Just like with the barre chords, this means that getting to know the scale numbers for both the E string AND the A string are essential (and with the root position seventh chords, we'll have to know the D string as well!).

The 3 chord is spelled 3, 5, 7, 2.

Remember that the scale "pattern number" comes from the note that your 1st finger starts with on the E string (not the A string or D string).

And, of course, remember that with quartal harmony (seventh chords):
1 and 4 chords = major7 chords    2, 3, and 6 chords = minor7 chords
5 chords = dominant7 chords    7 chords = minor7b5 chords

# THE "4" SEVENTH CHORD IN "G" MAJOR
## (Root on A string)

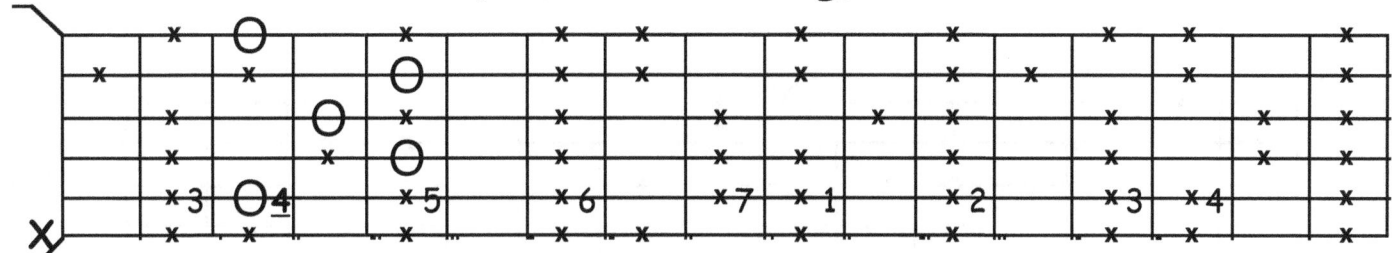

### Close up of "4" chord in pattern 7

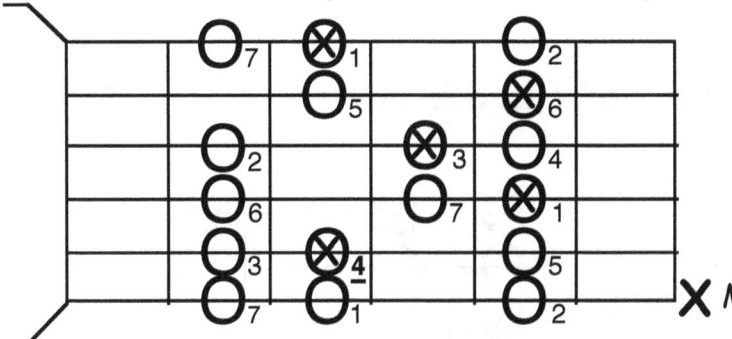

X Muffle low E string

The 4 chord is spelled: 4, 6, 1, 3.

# THE "5" SEVENTH CHORD IN "G" MAJOR
## (Root on A string)

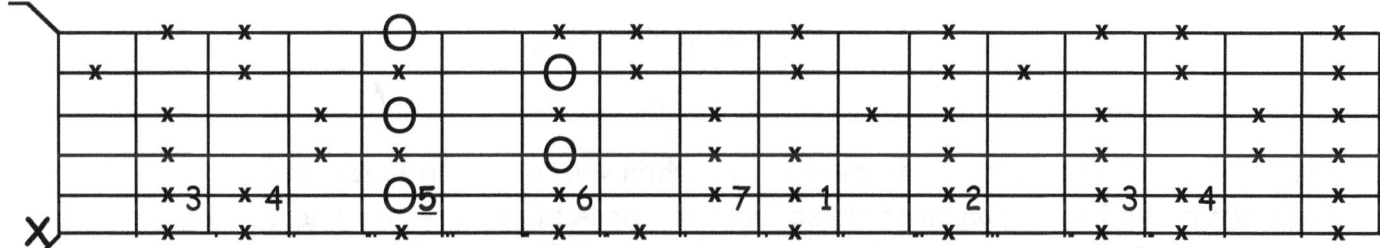

### Close up of "5" chord in pattern 2

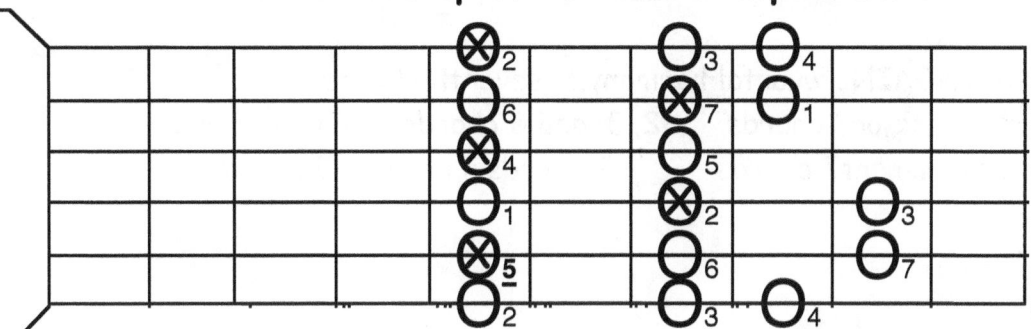

X Muffle low E string

The 5 chord is spelled: 5, 7, 2, 4. Remember that with quartal harmony (seventh chords):
  1 and 4 chords = major7 chords     2, 3, and 6 chords = minor7 chords
  5 chords = dominant7 chords        7 chords = minor7b5 chords

# THE "6" SEVENTH CHORD IN "G" MAJOR
## (Root on A string)

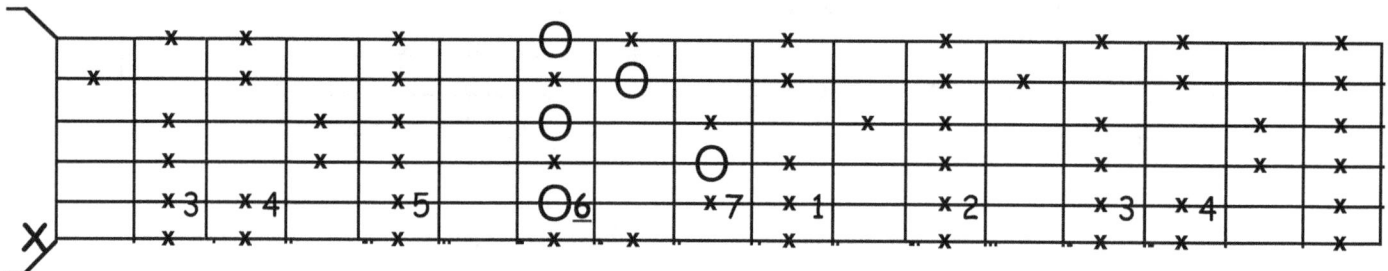

**Close up of "6" chord in pattern 3**

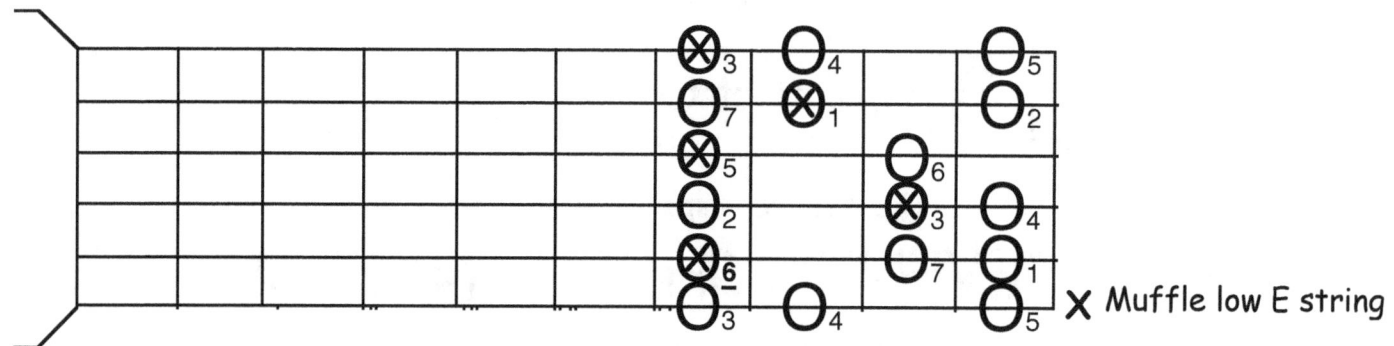

X Muffle low E string

The 6 chord is spelled: 6, 1, 3, 5.

ALSO remember to muffle that low E string when you're playing these chords. I've been reminding you on all of these "root on the A string seventh chord" diagrams, but soon I'll run out of room again on the right... so...

AND AGAIN... quartal harmony... (seventh chords):
1 and 4 chords = major7 chords     2, 3, and 6 chords = minor7 chords
5 chords = dominant7 chords         7 chords = minor7b5 chords

# THE "7" SEVENTH CHORD IN "G" MAJOR
## (Root on A string)

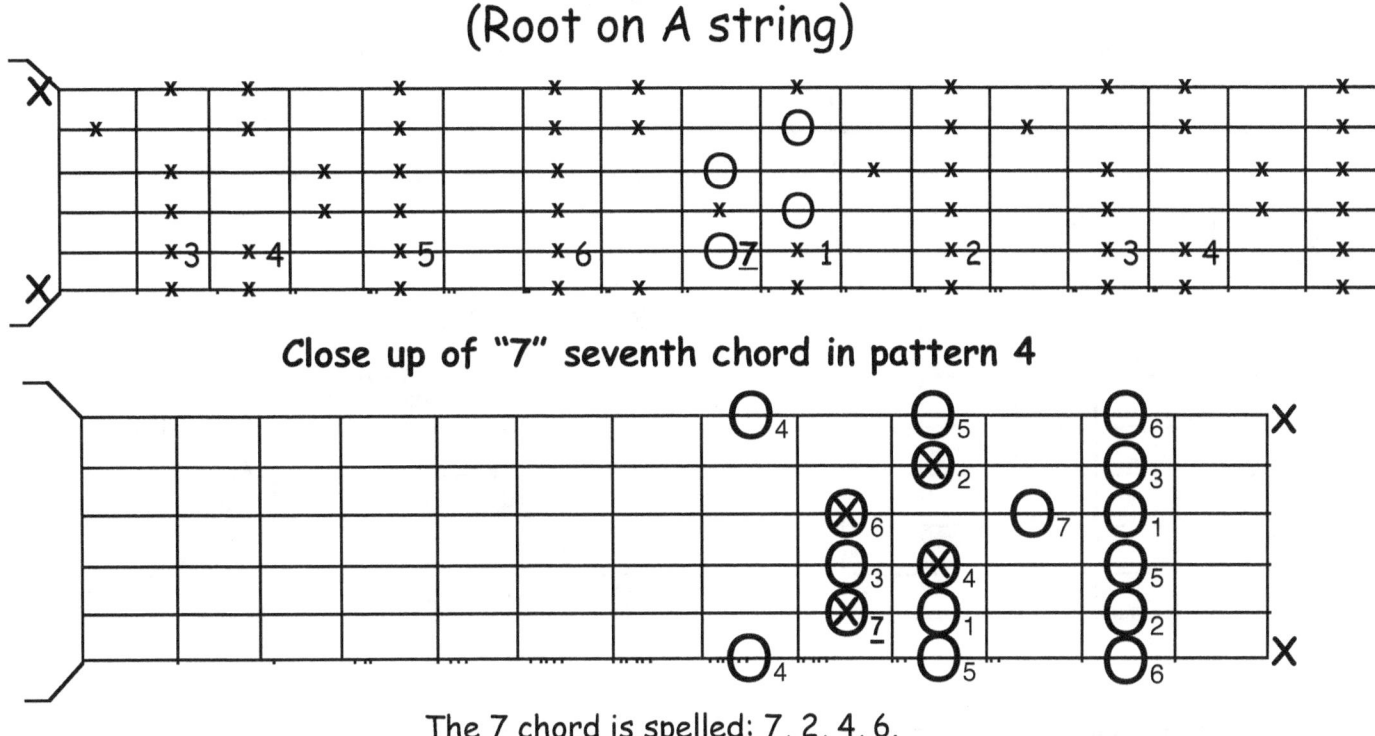

The 7 chord is spelled: 7, 2, 4, 6.

You'll have to muffle both the low E string AND the high E string with this voicing. The low E string can be muffled with the tip of the 1st finger of the left hand. The high E string can be muffled with the bottom part of the same 1st finger of your left hand. Just bring your hand close enough to the neck of the guitar that the base of the 1st finger touches the bottom of the neck and muffles the high E string.

If you're good, you can actually double the "b5" of this minor7b5 chord (the "4" of the G major scale is the b5 of this chord) by leaning in on the neck with this same bottom part of your left hand, first finger. This chord voicing would look like this:

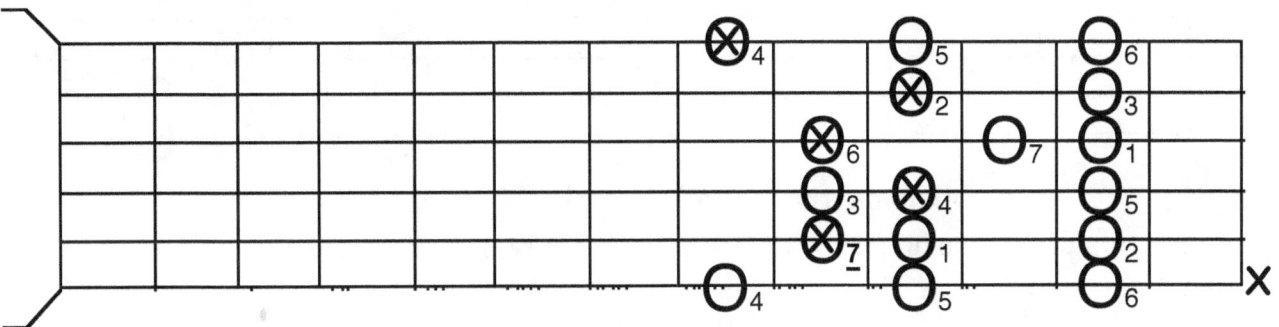

# THE "1" SEVENTH CHORD IN "G" MAJOR
## (Root on A string)

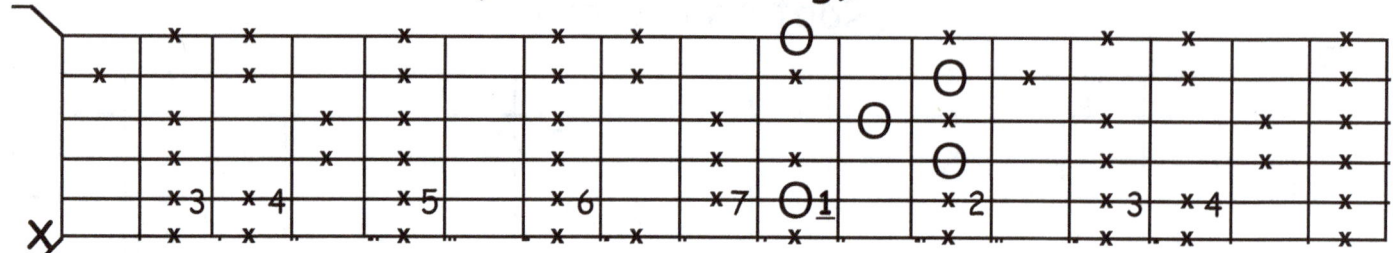

### Close up of "1" chord in pattern 4

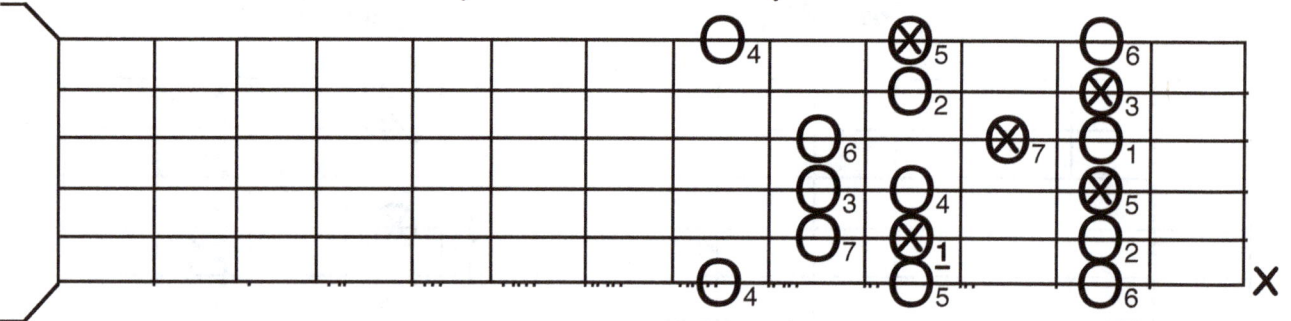

The 1 chord is spelled: 1, 3, 5, 7.

# THE "2" SEVENTH CHORD IN "G" MAJOR
## (Root on A string)

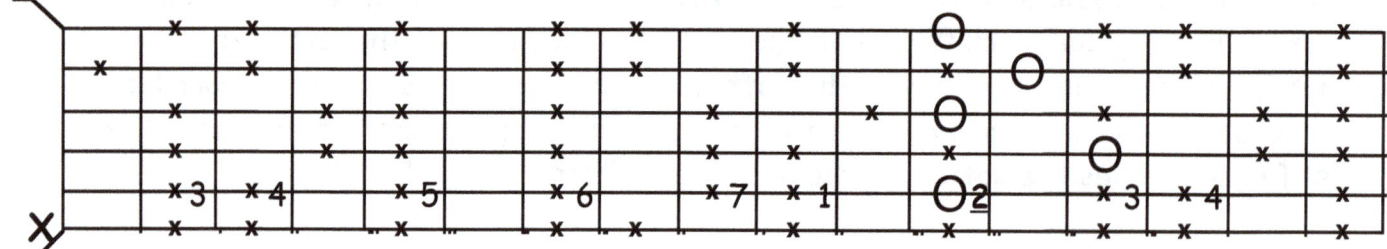

### Close up of "2" chord in pattern 6

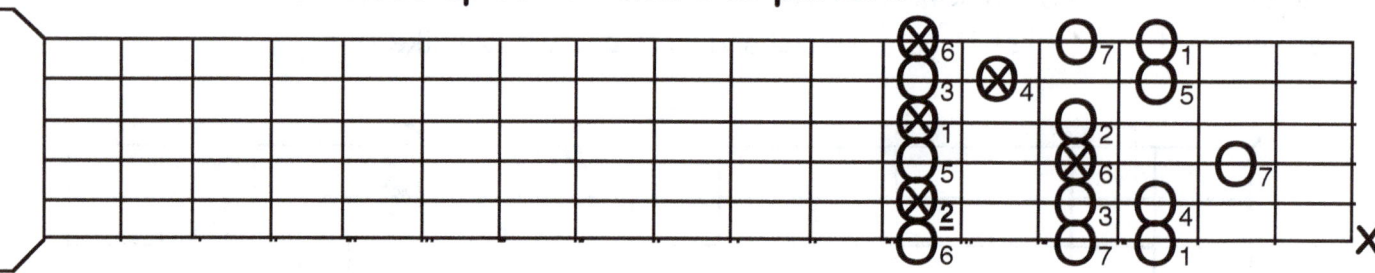

And yes, the 2 chord is spelled 2, 4, 6, 1.
At this point, you are remembering the tonality of the seventh chords...
1 and 4 chords = ?     2, 3, and 6 chords = ?     5 chords = ?     7 chords = ?
And you are, of course, muffling the low E string when you're playing these
"root on the A string" seventh chords... right? ... just checking.

# ROOT ON "D" STRING
## (Top 4 Strings)

## THE "6" SEVENTH CHORD IN "G" MAJOR

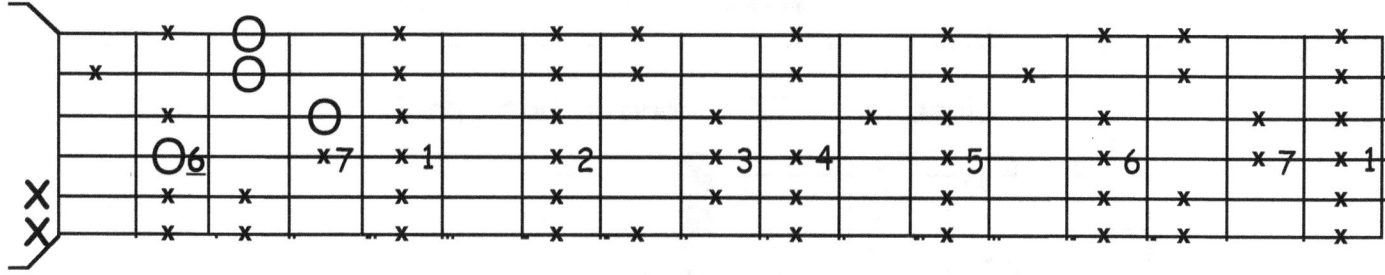

**Close up of "6" chord in pattern 7**

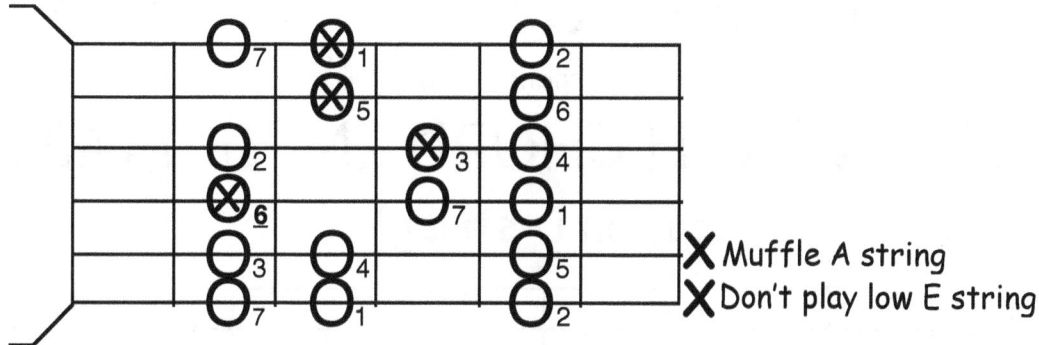

X Muffle A string
X Don't play low E string

At this point, you remember that the "scale pattern number" comes from the note that your 1st finger starts with on the E string (not the D string).

Once again, remember that a 6 chord is spelled: 6, 1, 3, 5.

And here, again, all of the quartal harmony (seventh chords) have these tonalities:

    1 and 4 chords = major7 chords      2, 3, and 6 chords = minor7 chords
       5 chords = dominant7 chords          7 chords = minor7b5 chords

# THE "7" SEVENTH CHORD IN "G" MAJOR
## (Root on D string)

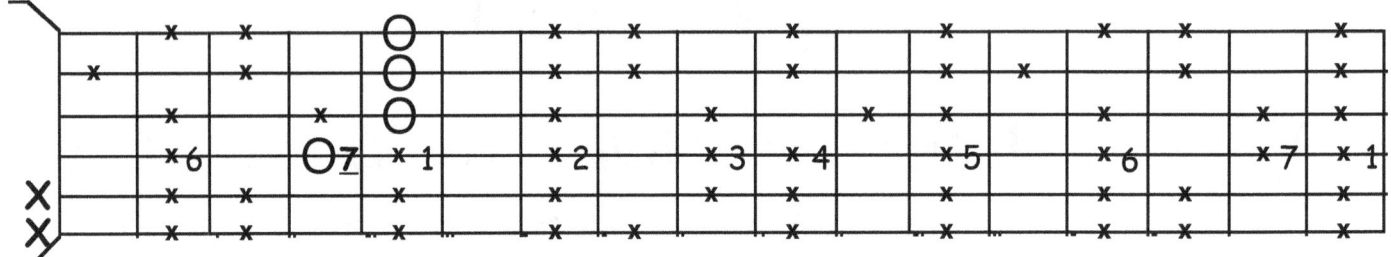

### Close up of "7" chord in pattern 7

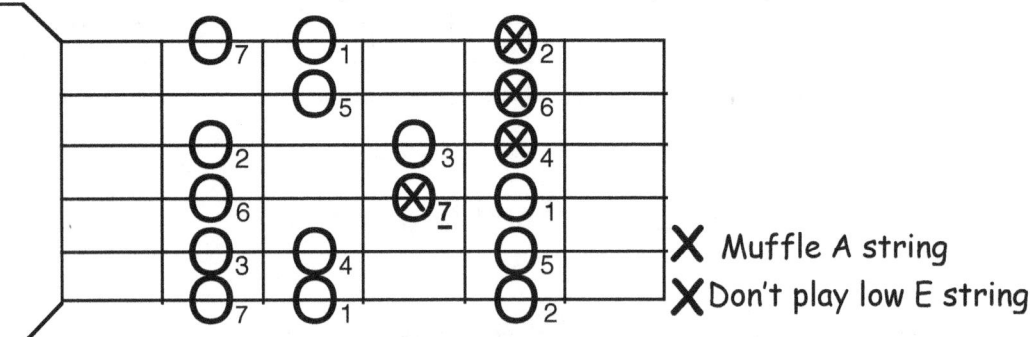

X Muffle A string
X Don't play low E string

The 7 chord is spelled: 7, 2, 4, 6.

# THE "1" SEVENTH CHORD IN "G" MAJOR
## (Root on D string)

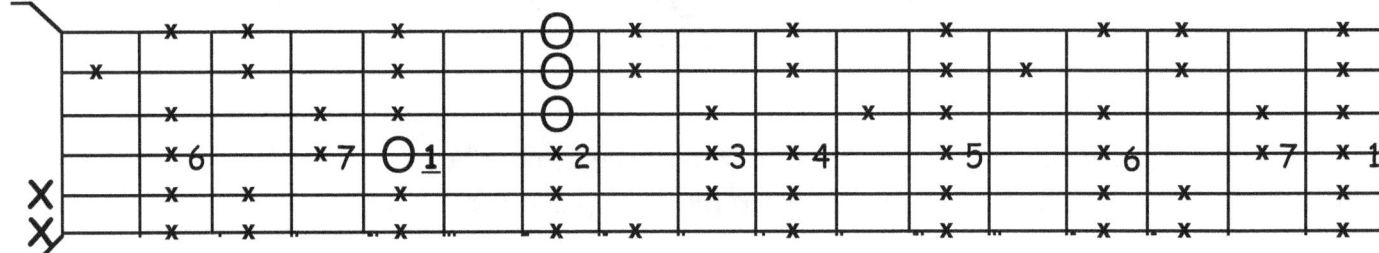

### Close up of "1" chord in pattern 2

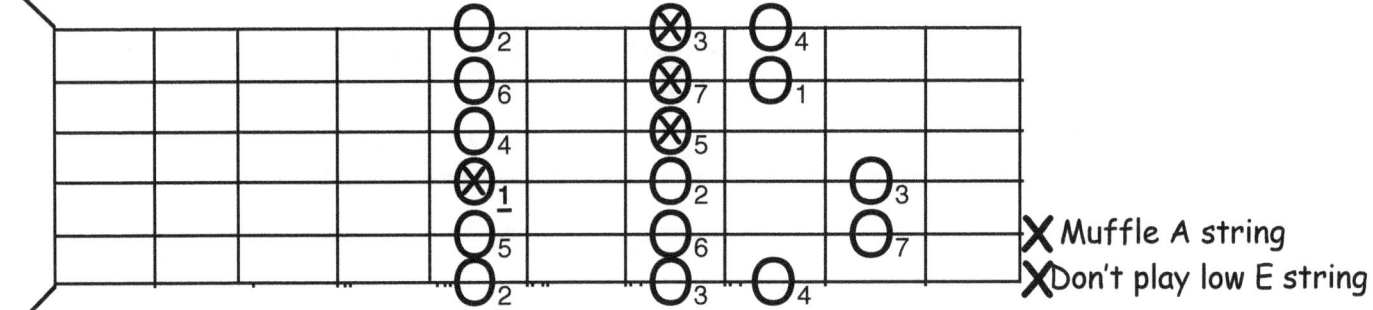

X Muffle A string
X Don't play low E string

The 1 chord is spelled 1, 3, 5, 7 and remember that the "scale pattern number" comes from the note that your 1st finger starts with on the low E string (not the D string). And, of course, you remember the tonalities for the quartal harmony (seventh chords)....

# THE "2" SEVENTH CHORD IN "G" MAJOR
## (Root on D string)

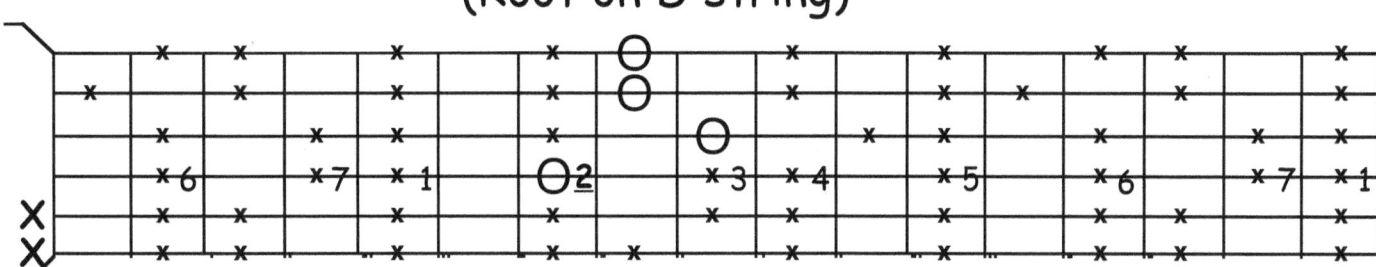

### Close up of "2" chord in pattern 3

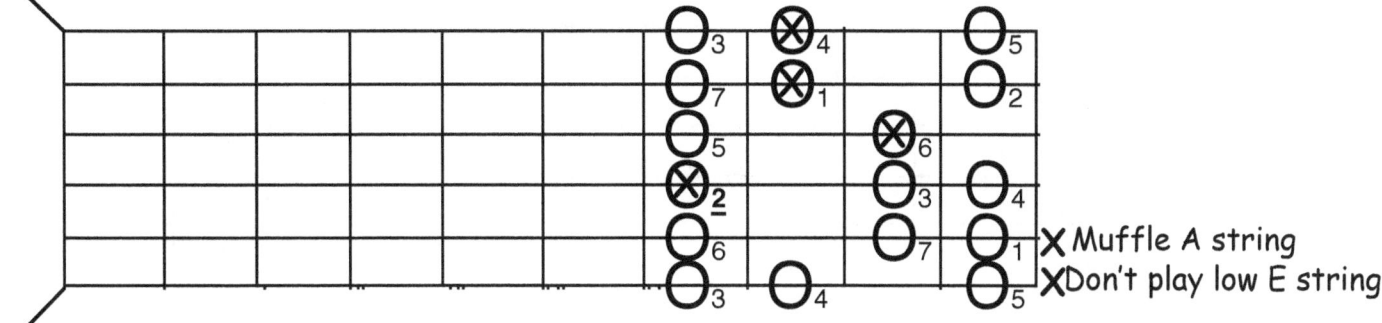

Yeah, yeah, yeah, 2, 4, 6, 1...

# THE "3" SEVENTH CHORD IN "G" MAJOR
## (Root on D string)

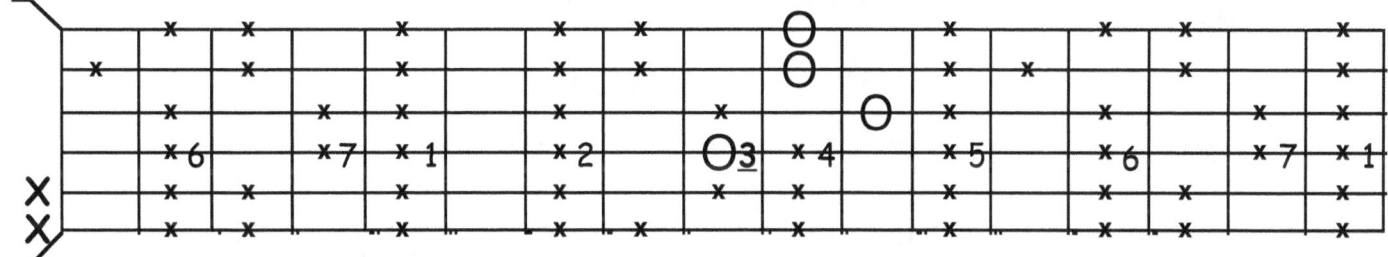

### Close up of "3" chord in pattern 4

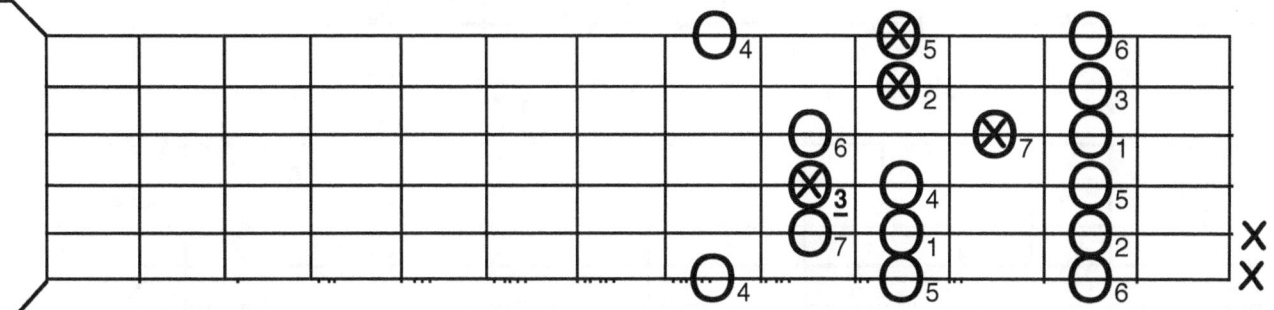

...the "scale pattern number" comes from the note that your 1st finger starts with on the E string (not the D string). I know that you know how to spell out the numbers for a 3 chord ...and, of course, you know what the tonality of a "3" chord is...

# THE "4" SEVENTH CHORD IN "G" MAJOR
## (Root on D string)

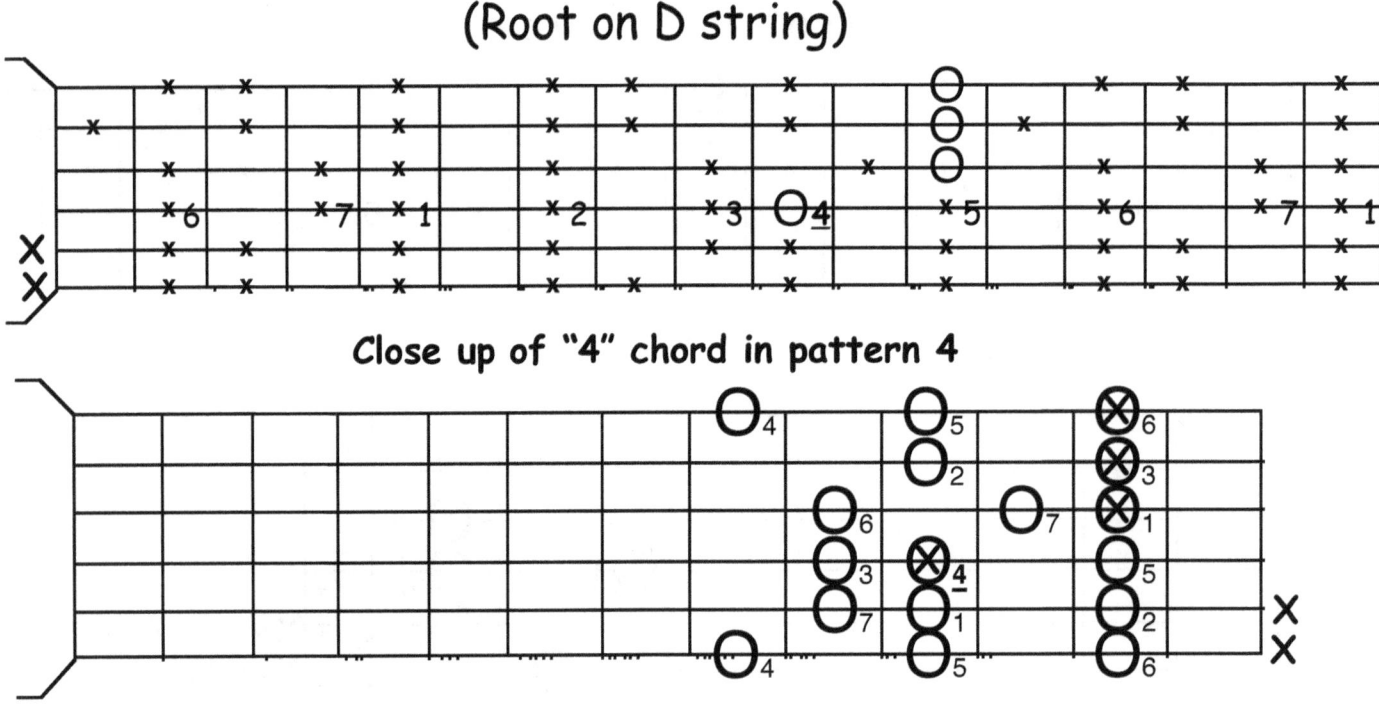

Close up of "4" chord in pattern 4

Numbers, numbers, numbers... Tonalities, tonalities, tonalities...

# THE "5" SEVENTH CHORD IN "G" MAJOR
## (Root on D string)

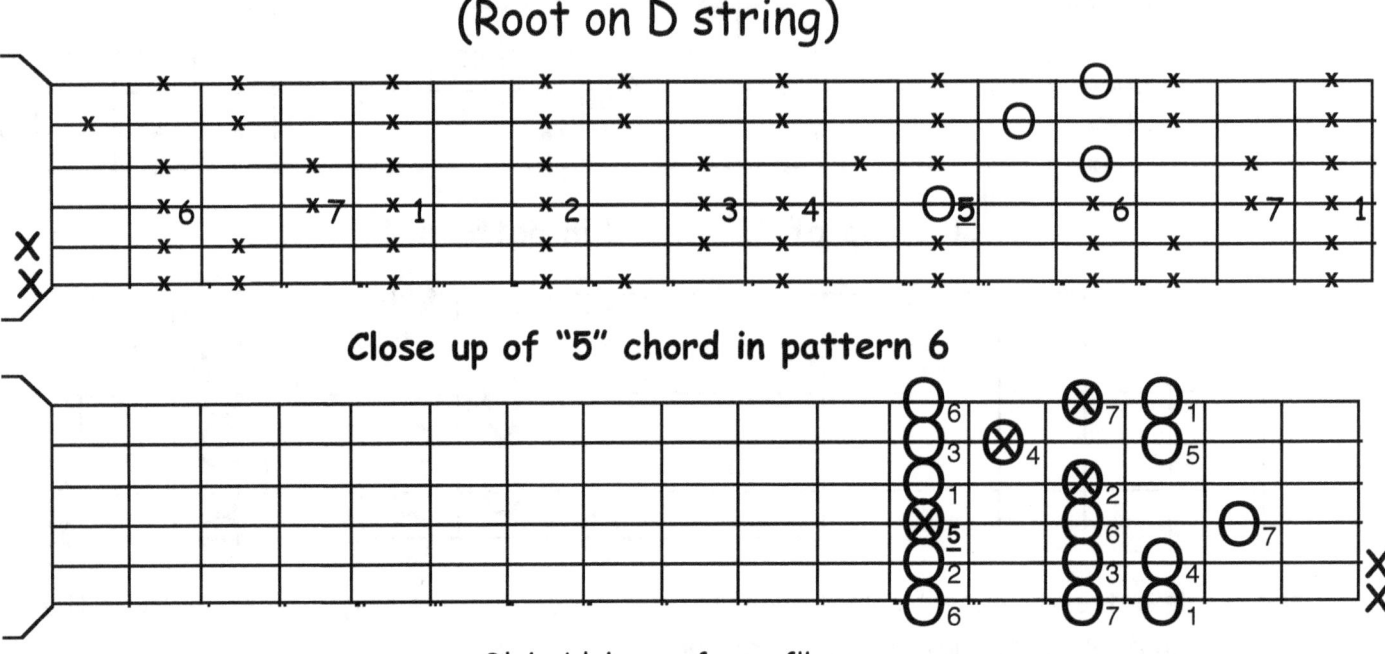

Close up of "5" chord in pattern 6

Blah, blah, woof, woof!!

Now that you have 3 different sets of 7th chords, you need an opportunity to use them. Below is a chord chart to try out these new chords.

First try playing all 3 voicings for each of the chords that are given: Fmaj7 with the root on the low E string, Fmaj7 with the root on the A string, and Fmaj7 with the root on the D string. Then Eb7 with the root on the low E string, Eb7 with the root on the A string etc... Do this for each chord. This will give you practice remembering the shapes of the voicings AND it will give you practice remembering where all of these letter names are on the low E, the A and the D strings.

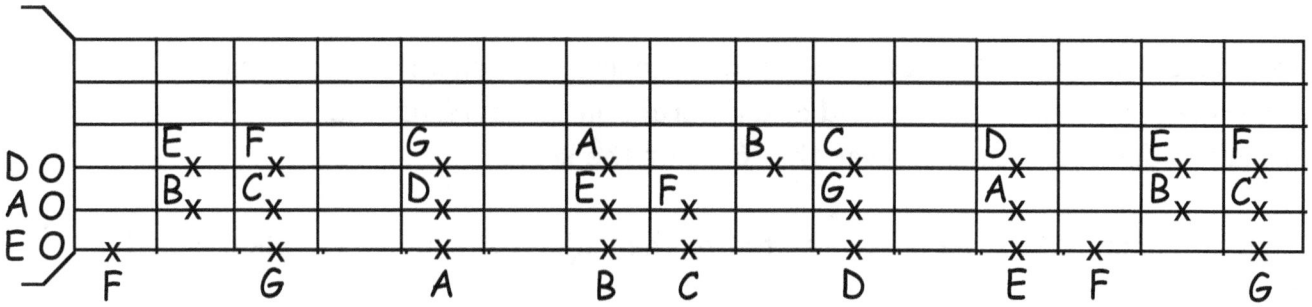

After this, try playing through the tune "in time" (keep an even beat or pulse). Play each chord only for the number of beats that is shown on the chart. Try mixing up the string groupings that you use to play through this chart so that you don't have to move your left hand too much when switching from chord to chord.

## DAYS OF 7TH CHORDS

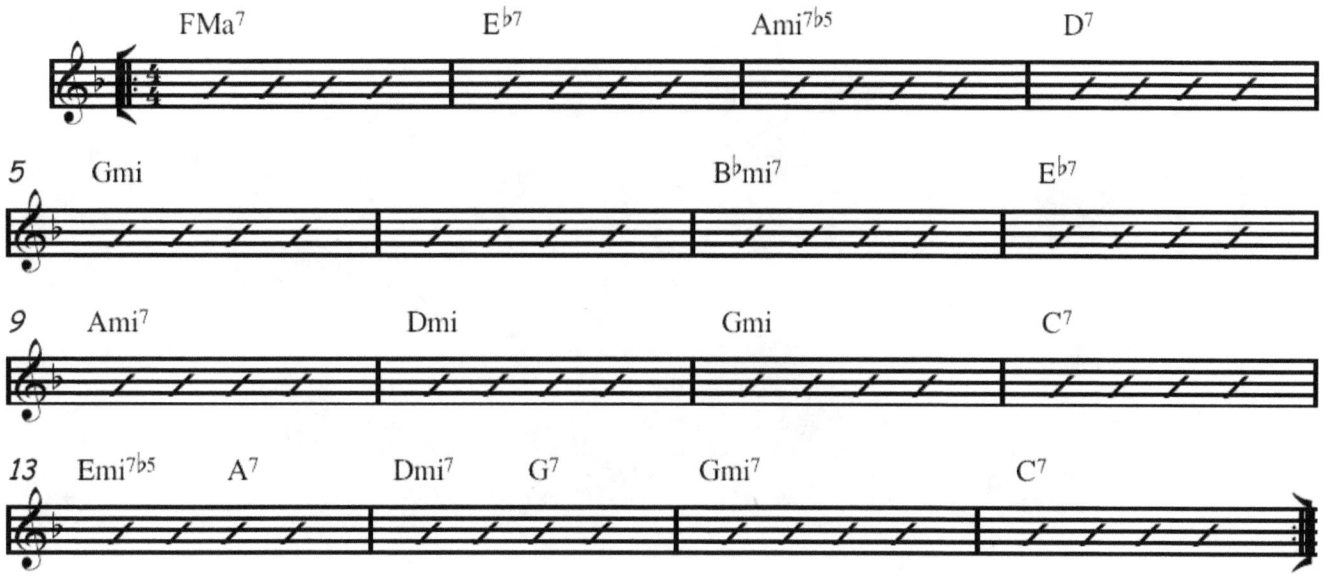

# "HARMONIC MINOR"

Today there are three different minor scales that are most commonly used when improvising:

1) <u>Natural or Pure minor</u>  You already know this one.  It is the relative minor of the major scale and it uses the same patterns as the major scale.  But remember that the minor scale name is derived from whatever the "6" is and the major scale name is derived from whatever the "1" is.

2) <u>Harmonic minor</u>  This is what we're about to learn.  It is also the relative minor of the major scale BUT it has a #5 instead of a natural 5 in its patterns.  Here too the name of this scale is derived from whatever the "6" is of the scale.

3) <u>Melodic minor</u>  This scale is also related to the major scale, but we'll talk about this one later on in the book.

For those students who have had a traditional introduction to music theory, and this #5 business seems a bit strange, have no fear.  Here is an explanation of the traditional approach to harmonic minor as it relates to the Major Method approach to harmonic minor... on the next page.

# "MAJOR METHOD VS TRADITIONAL"
## (HARMONIC MINOR)

TRADITIONALLY, the harmonic minor scale is taught as being the same as a natural minor scale (major scale with a b3, b6, & b7) only the 7 is NOT flatted.

```
                    1   2  b3  4  5  b6 b7  1
E natural minor:    E   F#  G  A  B  C  D   E

                    1   2  b3  4  5  b6  7   1
E harmonic minor:   E   F#  G  A  B  C   D#  E
```

The MAJOR METHOD teaches the harmonic minor scale as being based on the 6th scale degree of the relative major scale but with all of the 5's sharped. This "5" that is being sharped, is the same 5 that was introduced with the major scale patterns. All of the harmonic minor patterns and numbers **remain the same** as the major scale patterns and numbers except that everytime you get to a 5, you sharp it (you raise it one fret).

```
              1  2  3  4  5  6  7  1
G major:      G  A  B  C  D  E  F# G

                    6   7  1  2  3  4  5   6
E natural minor:    E   F# G  A  B  C  D   E

                    6   7  1  2  3  4  #5  6
E harmonic minor:   E   F# G  A  B  C  D#  E
```

Since we are using all of the patterns and numbers from the major scale patterns, we can now learn all of the patterns of the harmonic minor scale fairly quickly. The harmonic minor scale shapes are **exactly the same** as the major scale shapes with one exception. All you have to do is "sharp" all of the 5th scale degrees. This gives you the harmonic minor shapes.

Remember that this G major scale with a sharped 5 is ALWAYS referred to by its minor name: "E harmonic minor". Learning the harmonic minor scale this way could be somewhat difficult and confusing for other instruments. But for guitarists, with the large visual labyrinth of shapes that we need to know just to play a simple major scale, this is the quickest and most efficient way to learn the harmonic minor scale. You will still have to "LISTEN" (with the ears) to these shapes (with the eyes) in order to make good music. So here now are the E harmonic patterns on the guitar....

# E "Harmonic Minor" Scale Shapes

The small numbers represent the relative <u>major</u> scale pitches:
1=G 2=A 3=B 4=C **#5=D#** 6=E 7=F#

## Pattern 7

This is still labeled as "Pattern 7" because it starts with the 7th scale degree of the relative <u>major</u> scale.

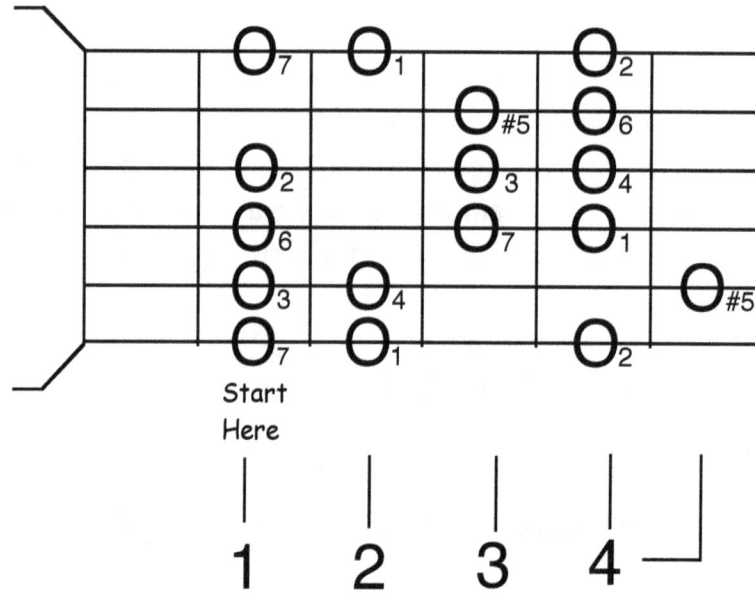

These larger numbers represent the left hand fingers that are used to play the notes on these particular frets... and, yes, you will have to stretch that 4th finger again.

\* No current music theorists refer to the E harmonic minor scale as the G major scale with a sharped 5th. However:

1) The two scales are identical.

2) On the guitar it takes so much to learn all of the major patterns on the entire neck of the guitar AND the harmonic minor sound is only one note away from all of those shapes that you've already learned (the #5 is the only difference).

Please keep in mind that this is raw information. You will still have to listen to the sound of these shapes to make good music out of them.

# E "Harmonic Minor" Scale Shapes
## Pattern 1

This is labeled as "Pattern 1" because it starts with the 1st relative <u>major</u> scale degree.

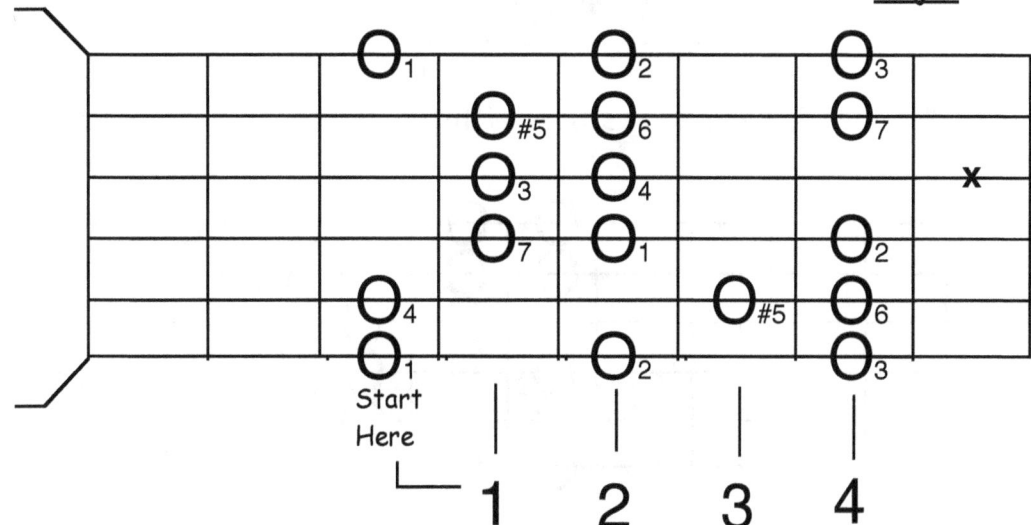

Ah yes, more first finger stretches. With this pattern, the 4th finger would have to stretch in order to play the #5 on the G or 3rd string (where the "x" appears). Because of the structure of the string tuning, you can also play this same note with your 1st finger on the B or 2nd string. Since this will eliminate the need for both a 1st finger stretch <u>and</u> a 4th finger stretch, go ahead and use your 1st finger on the B or 2nd string.

## Pattern 2

This is labeled as "Pattern 2" because it starts with the 2nd relative <u>major</u> scale degree.

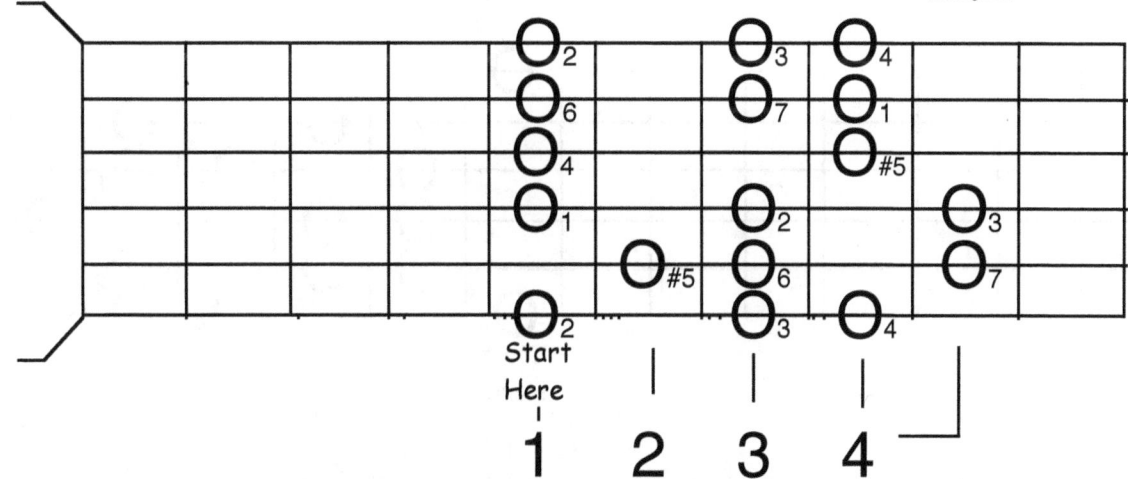

Note: I realize that using your 2nd finger for that #5 on the A or 5th string, followed by the 3rd finger and then the 4th finger stretch is a huge pain in the... neck (and its really tempting to slide your hand to the right for that string), but developing the independence and coordination of those lesser used fingers is important. This seems to be as good a time as any to work on these weaknesses.

# E "Harmonic Minor" Scale Shapes

## Pattern 3

This is labeled as "Pattern 3" because it starts with the 3rd relative <u>major</u> scale degree.

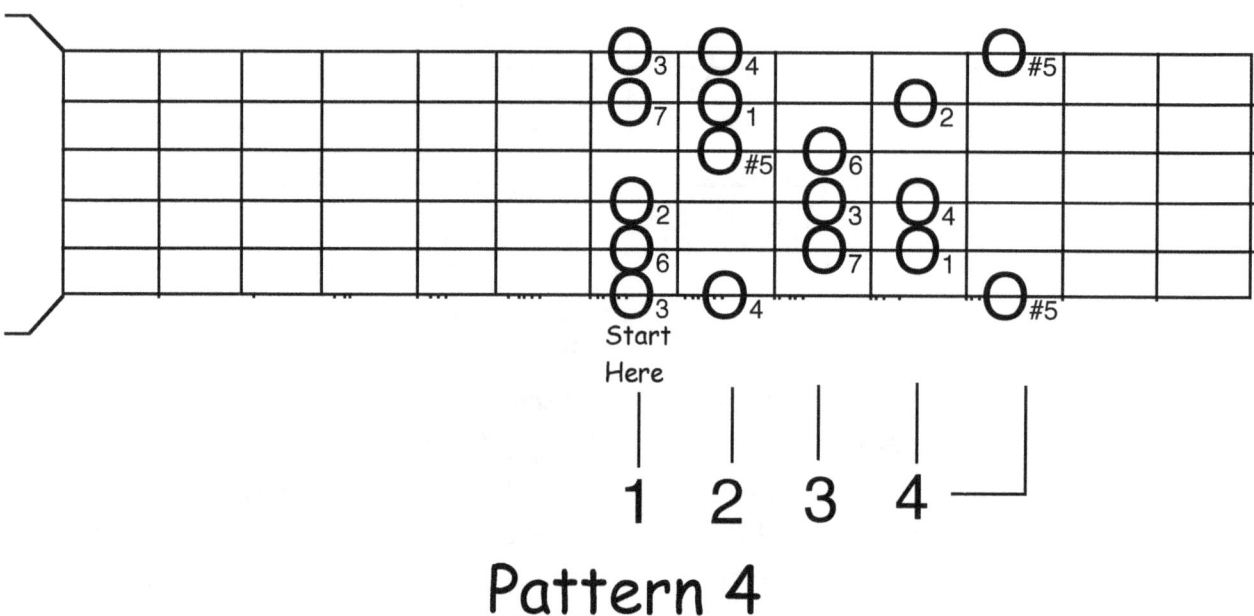

## Pattern 4

This is labeled as "Pattern 4" because it starts with the 4th relative <u>major</u> scale degree.

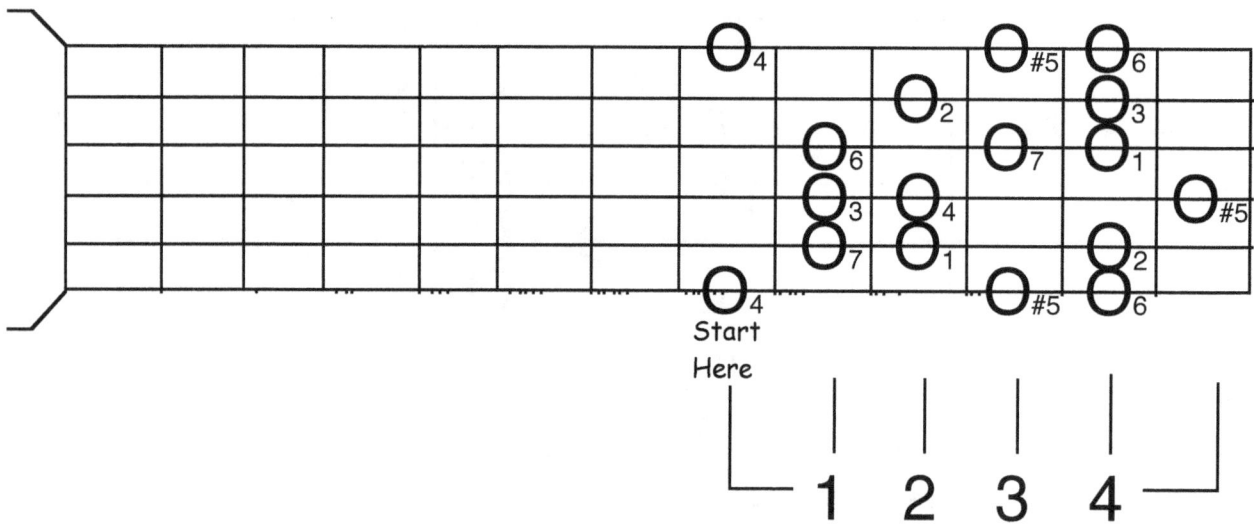

<u>Now</u>, not only another one of those pesky first finger stretches, but also a 4th finger stretch in the same pattern!!

# E "Harmonic Minor" Scale Shapes
## Pattern #5

This is labeled as "Pattern #5" because it starts with the #5th relative major scale degree.

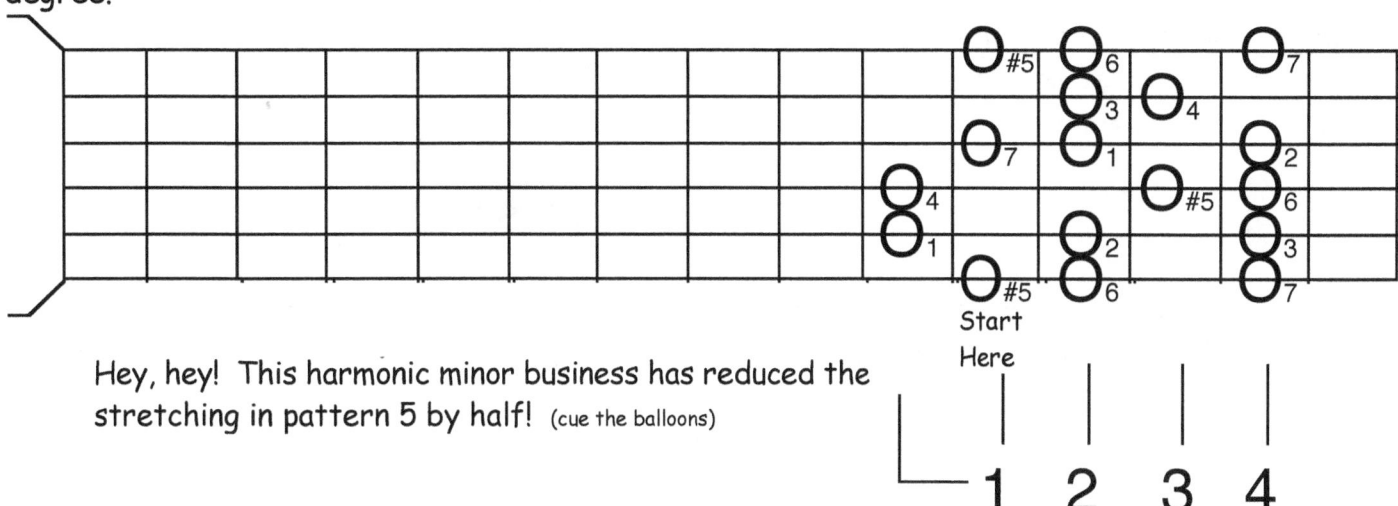

Hey, hey! This harmonic minor business has reduced the stretching in pattern 5 by half! (cue the balloons)

## Pattern 6

This is labeled as "Pattern 6" because it starts with the 6th relative major scale degree.

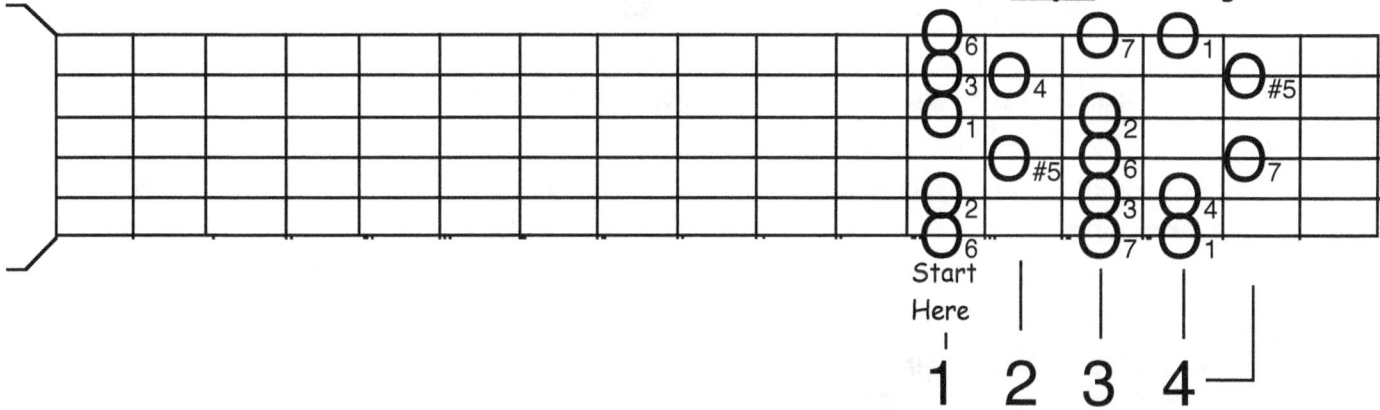

Here's what the entire harmonic minor neck looks like around pattern 6

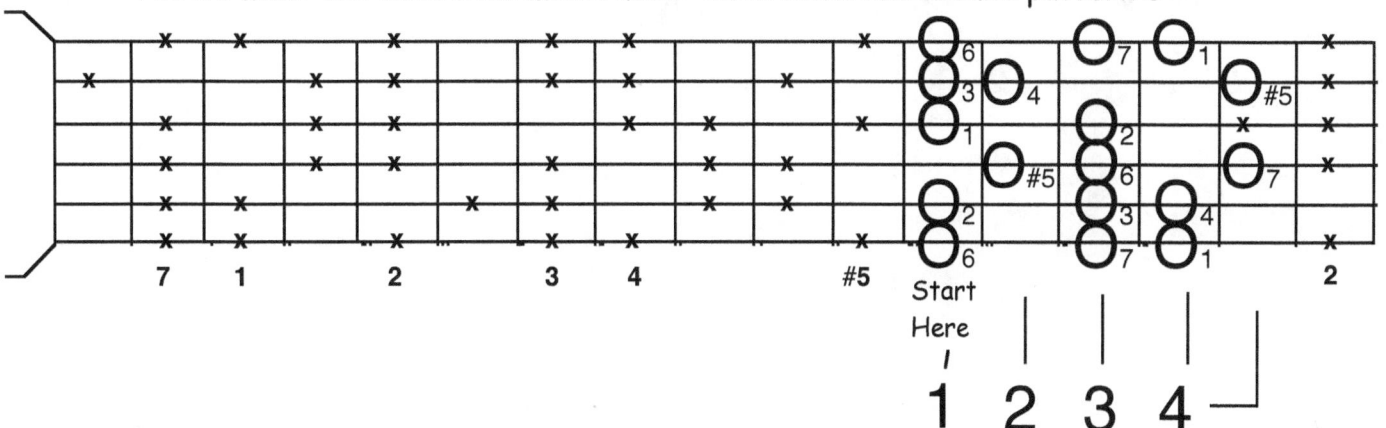

80

Once you've gotten the harmonic minor shapes down, you've tied them together, and you can solo in E harmonic minor all over the neck, staying in key and not getting lost (phew), you should transpose the whole thing into another key. This just means sliding everything up or down on the neck. Try doing this. Pick a new key, slide the number of frets you need to slide in order to play in this new key and begin soloing in this new key. Try to "see" the patterns without any blind spots. If you get lost, go back to a place on the neck where you know what pattern you should be in and keep playing. Figure out where you got lost before and work on that part of the neck to make sure that its solid the next time you're in that neighborhood.

## HOW DO YOU USE THIS SCALE?

There are many uses for the harmonic minor scale. And we'll deal with these uses in greater depth in... a future volume of the Major Method.

But, for now, I'll give you at least one way in which you can use this scale:

When you're given a dominant7 chord to solo over (the dominant7 chord is the chord built on the 5th scale degree of a major scale), instead of playing the major scale that the 5 chord comes from, you can play the harmonic minor scale that **shares the same letter name as the major scale** that the 5 chord comes from.

What this means is that if you are given a D dominant7 chord to solo over, rather than playing in the key of G major, you would solo in the key of G harmonic minor! This means that you no longer think of the G as the 1 for a major scale. You now think of the G as the 6 for the harmonic minor scale. I know, this seems like you're breaking the rules. But this kind of bending and breaking of the rules is part of what makes music so interesting. These kinds of mixing and matching of scales and chords are called chord-scale relationships. And, again, I'll deal with this stuff more in... a future volume.

For now, just get used to the harmonic minor patterns and learn them thoroughly.

# MELODIC MINOR

This is the last of the 3 minor scales that you'll have to know to get through most contemporary improvisational situations. Here again we'll relate this scale to the major patterns that you know OH SO WELL by now.

The melodic minor scale has evolved over the years. It used to be a scale that ascended with one set of notes and descended with another set of notes. This is still taught in traditional (common practice period) music theory classes. Its applications in today's musical environment are fairly limited.

The descending mode of this traditional melodic minor scale IS the natural minor scale. And as you no doubt remember, the patterns of the natural minor scale are exactly the same as the relative major scale shapes (...the shapes that you are now seeing in your sleep and transposing to different keys for soloing every day! ...right?)

The ascending mode of this traditional melodic minor is the part of the scale that provides for a new set of shapes (and sounds) on the neck. Today, this is the part of the scale that is widely referred to as the melodic minor scale (except, of course, if you are studying for an exam in common practice period music theory).

As luck would have it, and as I mentioned earlier, this scale can be related back to the major scale shapes (more balloons!). There are a couple of ways to see/hear this scale on the neck. When I learned this scale, I happened to choose the road less traveled... I now know why it is the road less traveled and we're not going down that road (More about this less traveled road later).

Today's melodic minor scale is THE SAME as the major scale with a flatted 3rd scale degree. So now we have to go back to all of those major scale patterns and redraw all 7 shapes with a b3 instead of the regular 3.

The other great news about this scale is that the letter name of the scale stays the same as with the major scale!! So the G major scale with a flatted 3, IS the G melodic minor scale.

And, again, while it may be tempting to try and just wing it with knowing this scale (playing the majors and just trying to flat the 3's as they come up), you really have to see/hear this scale as a whole new sound. Get to know these shapes independently as the melodic minor scale... and for those more familiar with the "traditional" approach:

# "MAJOR METHOD VS TRADITIONAL"
## (MELODIC MINOR)

TRADITIONALLY, the melodic minor scale ascends with one set of notes and descends with another set of notes. The ascending scale (mode) is the same as the natural minor scale with the 6th & 7th scale degrees raised by a half step. The descending melodic minor scale lowers these scale degress back, meaning that the descending mode is the same as the natural minor scale.

```
                          1  2   3  4 5  6  7  1
                E major:  E  F#  G# A B  C# D# E

                          1  2   b3 4 5  b6 b7 1
        E natural minor:  E  F#  G  A B  C  D  E

                              1  2  b3 4 5 6  7  1
E melodic minor (ascending mode): E F# G  A B C# D# E
```

When looking at this scale, one realizes that the ascending mode of the melodic minor is the SAME as the major scale with a b3... so the MAJOR METHOD teaches the melodic minor scale as the same as a major scale with a b3. All of the patterns and numbers remain the same except that everytime you get to a 3, you flat it (you lower it one fret).

```
                         1  2   3  4 5  6  7  1
               E major:  E  F#  G# A B  C# D# E

                         1  2   b3 4 5  6  7  1
       E melodic minor:  E  F#  G  A B  C# D# E
```

With the Major Method, you only have to change one note per octave, and you're good to go! Just keep in mind that with the Major Method, the melodic minor scale and the major scale that you use to learn it, share the same letter name. G melodic minor scale is **the same** as the G major scale with a b3.

So here now are the G melodic minor patterns on the guitar....

# G "Melodic Minor" Scale Shapes

The small numbers represent the scale pitches:
1=G 2=A b3=Bb 4=C 5=D 6=E 7=F#

## Pattern 7

This is labeled as "Pattern 7" because it starts with the 7th scale degree.

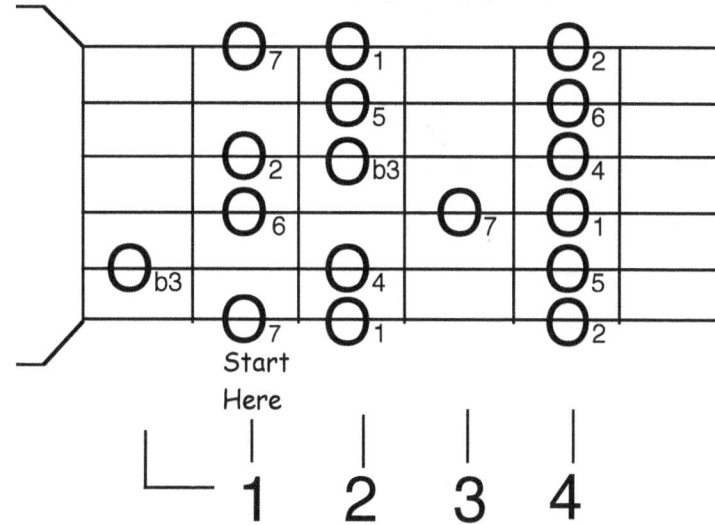

These larger numbers represent the left hand fingers that are used to play the notes on these frets (note that the thumb is not considered a finger on the left hand .... and, yes, you've heard all this before... AND you've got another one of those 1st finger stretches).

## Pattern 1

This is labeled as "Pattern 1" because it starts with the 1st scale degree.

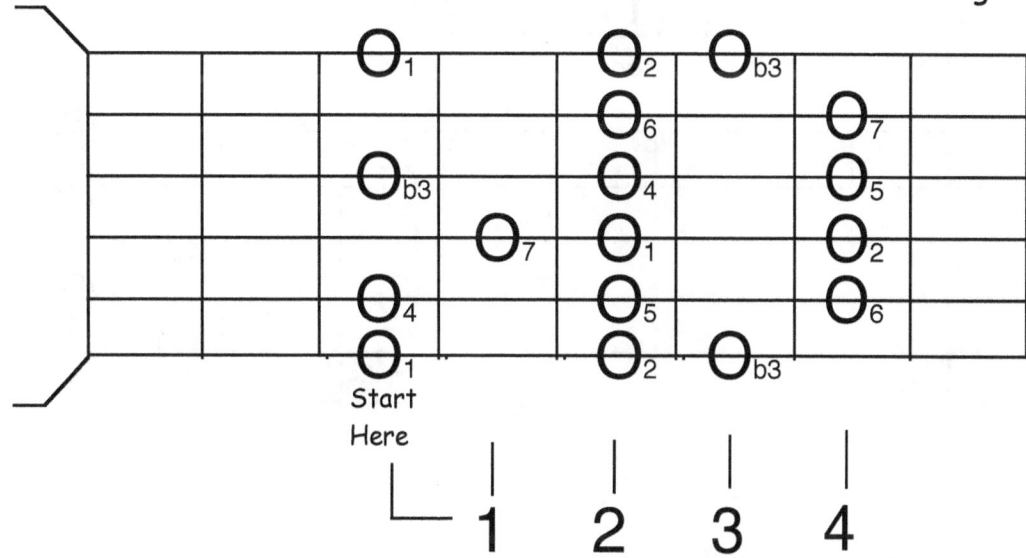

The first finger must "stretch" to play the notes on the third fret. Note: when doing this, make sure that you still use your 2nd finger for the notes on the 5th fret, your 3rd finger for the notes on the 6th fret, and your 4th finger for the notes on the 7th fret.

# G "Melodic Minor" Scale Shapes

## Pattern 2

This is labeled as "Pattern 2" because it starts with the 2nd scale degree.

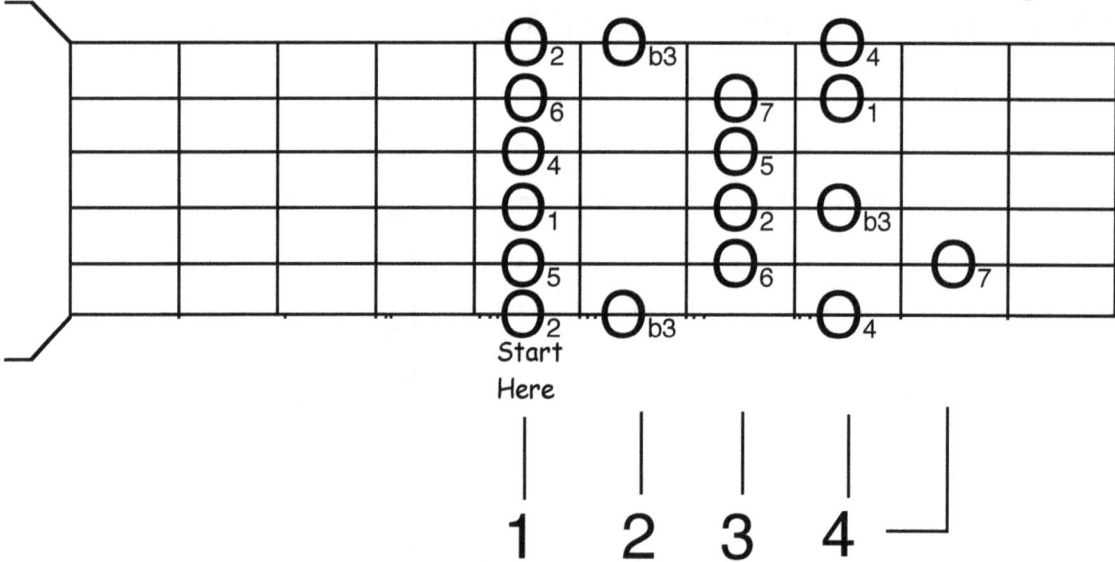

The 4th finger must "stretch" to play the note on the 9th fret of the A string. Note: when doing this, make sure that you still use your 3rd finger for the notes on the 7th fret, your 2nd finger for the notes on the 6th fret, and your 1st finger for the notes on the 5th fret.

## Pattern b3

This is labeled as "Pattern b3" because it starts with the b3rd scale degree.

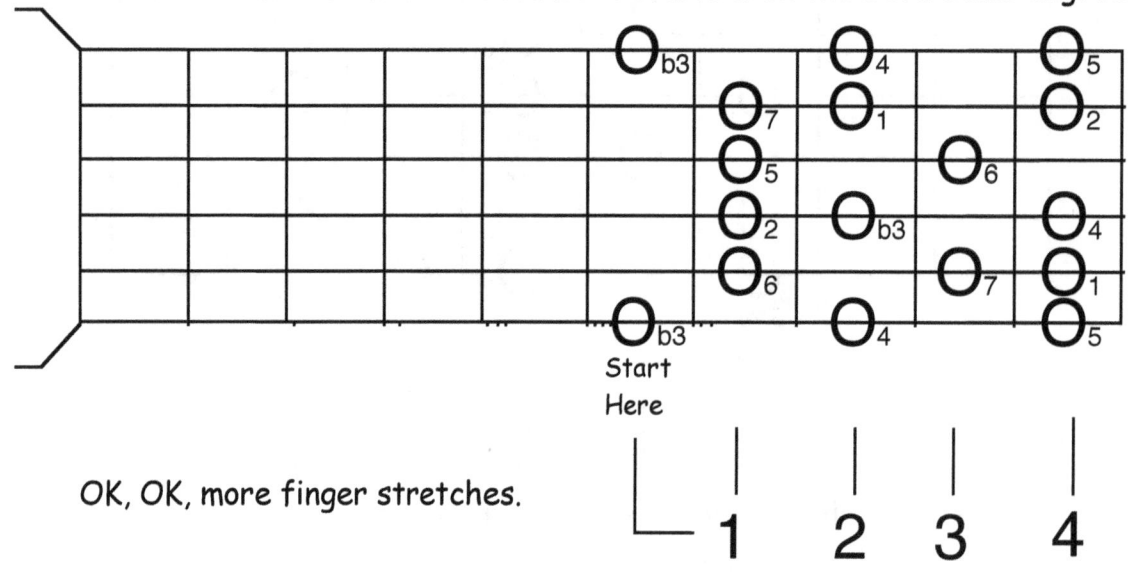

OK, OK, more finger stretches.

# G "Melodic Minor" Scale Shapes
## Pattern 4

This is labeled as "Pattern 4" because it starts with the 4th scale degree.

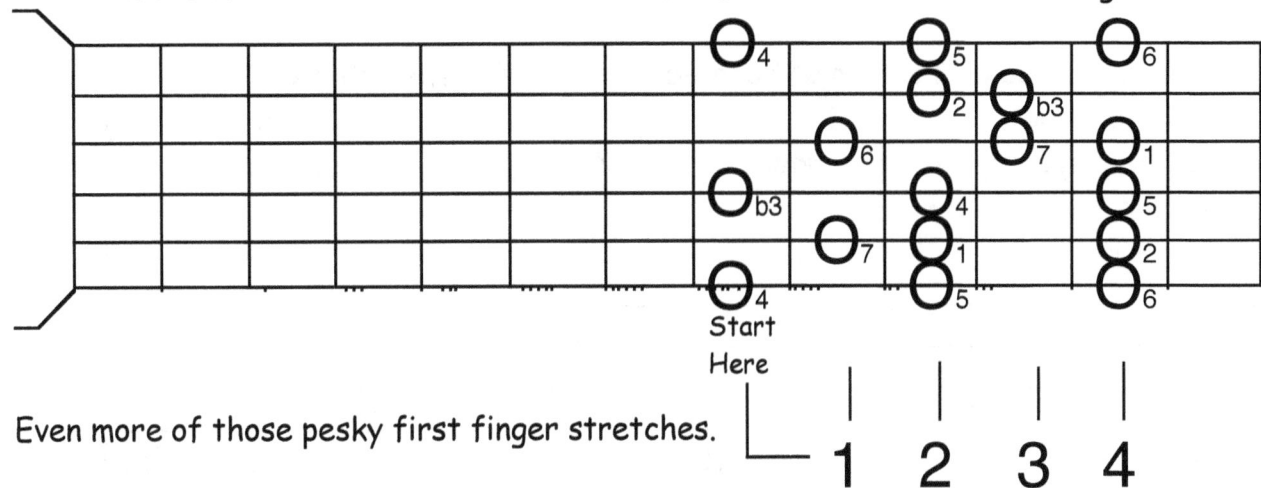

Even more of those pesky first finger stretches.

## Pattern 5

This is labeled as "Pattern 5" because it starts with the 5th scale degree.

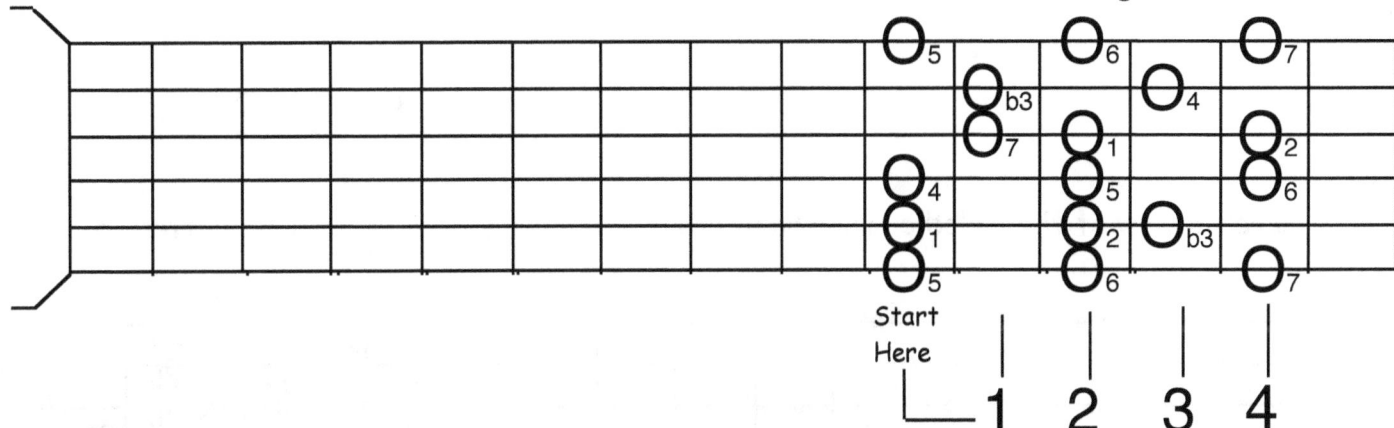

And yes, there are other ways of fingering these patterns, like this:

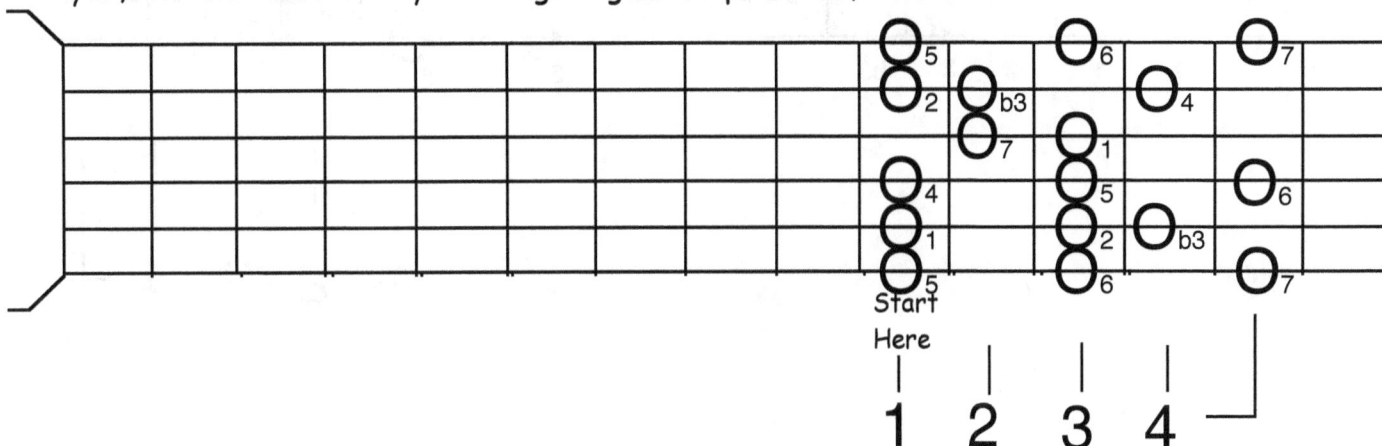

# G "Melodic Minor" Scale Shapes

## Pattern 6

This is labeled as "Pattern 6" because it starts with the 6th scale degree. Because of the structure of the string tuning, the b3 that appears on the 2nd string (x) can now be played by the 4th finger on the 3rd string, there-by avoiding yet another finger stretch.

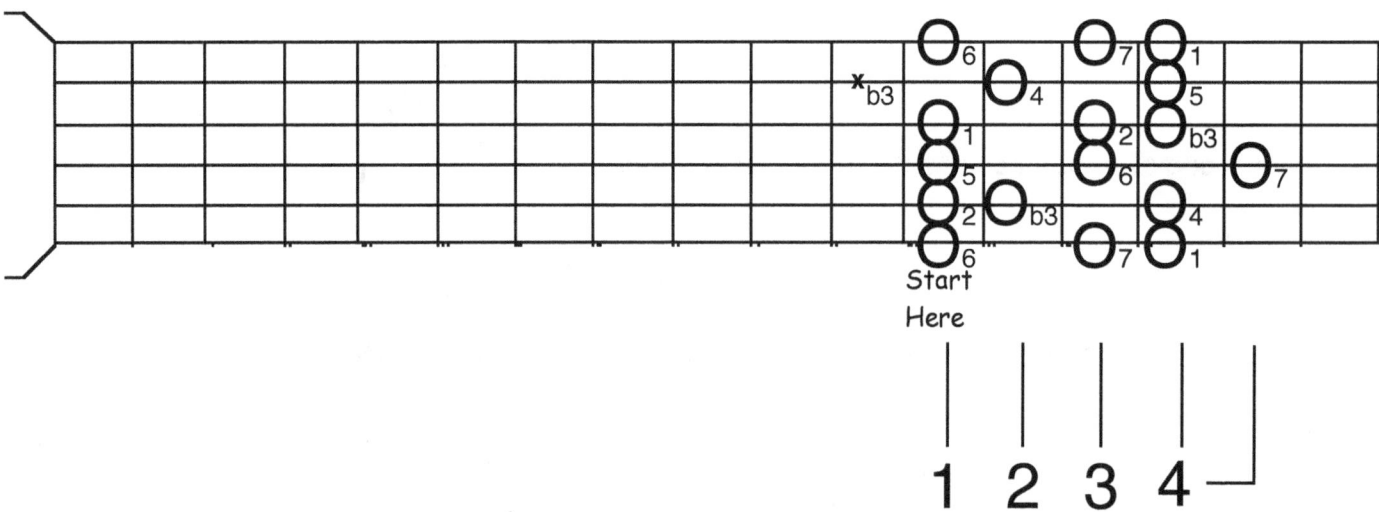

Here's a view of the melodic minor patterns on the entire neck set around pattern 6:

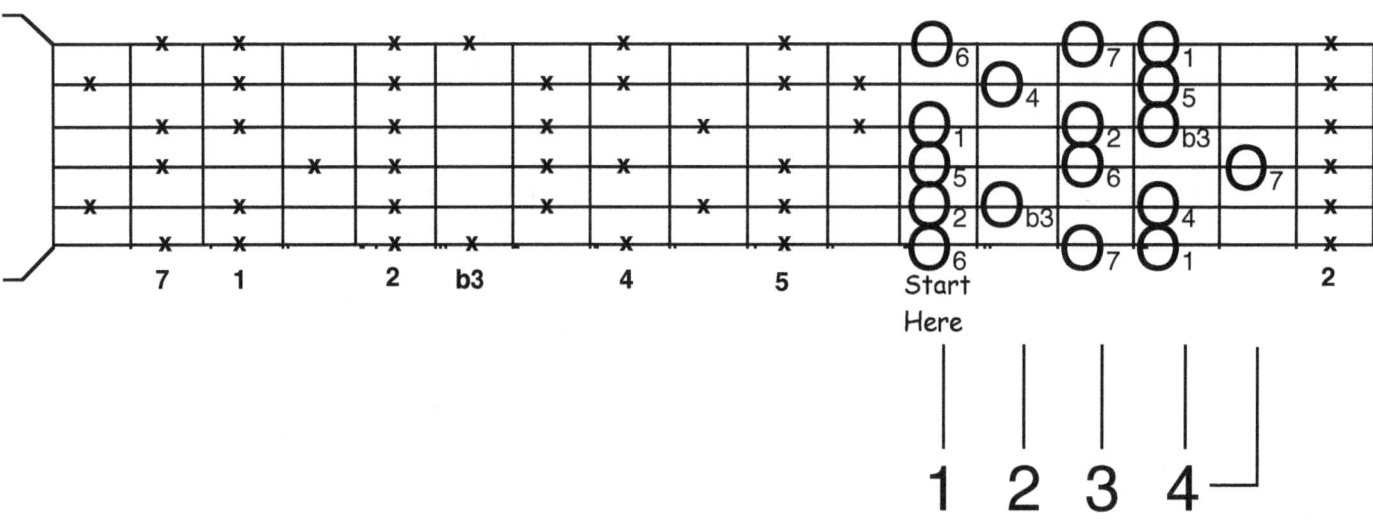

Once you've gotten the melodic minor shapes down, you've tied them together, and you can solo in G melodic minor all over the neck, staying in key and not getting lost (phew again), you should transpose the whole thing into another key. This just means sliding everything up or down on the neck. Try doing this. Pick a new key, slide the number of frets you need to slide in order to play in this new key and begin soloing in this new key. Try to "see" the patterns without any blind spots. If you get lost, go back to a place on the neck where you know what pattern you should be in and keep playing. Figure out where you got lost before and work on that part of the neck to make sure that its solid the next time you're in that neighborhood... (does this paragraph sound familiar?)

## HOW DO YOU USE THIS SCALE?

There are many uses for the melodic minor scale. Perhaps even more than for the harmonic minor. For now, I'll give you at least one way in which you can use this scale:

When you're given a dominant7 chord to solo over (a chord built on the 5th scale degree of a major scale) instead of playing the major scale that the 5 chord comes from, you can play the melodic minor scale that comes from the 5th of that dominant7 chord (we'll talk more about this "5th of the 5 chord" business in the cycle of 5ths section of this book).

What this means is that if you are given a D dominant7 chord (D7) to solo over, rather than playing in the key of G major, you would figure out what the 5 of the "D" chord is. The 5 of D is A. So you would solo in A melodic minor. This all might seem like a lot of mental gymnastics right now, but as you become more familiar with the cycle of fifths and the sounds that these rules create, you'll become much more comfortable with the rules themselves.

And don't forget that you can always come up with other ways of thinking about music theory that may make things easier for you. For instance, if you want to play that same melodic minor scale over that same D7 chord, you can just play the melodic minor that is based on the 2nd scale degree in G major. In other words:

1) Figure out what key the dominant7 chord comes from.
2) Play the melodic minor scale starting on the 2nd scale degree of this key.

This way of thinking will give you the exact same results as the 5 of 5 business that I mentioned earlier. Its just a different way of getting to the same place. Of course, once you know your cycle of fifths (which gives you all of the 5th relationships), figuring out the 5 of the 5 may be easier and quicker. You will just have to decide for yourself which method you'll use to organize this theory in your head.

Soon you will be able to figure out what key a dominant7 chord comes from very quickly. It is one of the most common chord types and it is used all over the place. Remember that there are only 12 different keys (and some of them are just sharped or flatted versions of the natural keys: G is the 5 of C ...AND G# is the 5 of C#, so its not going to be too difficult).

All of this mixing and matching of scales and chords (once again) is called chord-scale relationships. Your mission for now, is to get used to the melodic minor patterns and learn them thoroughly. But first...

# THE ROAD LESS TRAVELED

I wasn't going to include this information because it can cause some confusion and insight "minor" riots (no pun intended... but appreciated).

When learning the melodic minor scale, I was given a piece of paper with the scale written out in musical notation on a staff (the staff is the 5 lines that music is written on). I was told to learn this scale on the neck of the guitar and to transpose it into all 12 keys (courtesy of Steve Brown @ Ithaca College).

Well, I figured out that it was just the major scale with a flatted 3rd scale degree. But at that time, I didn't know where all of the 3's were within the major scale shapes. So (take a deep breath and hang on here), I further analyzed that this scale *could* be "seen" as a major scale with a sharped 1. And since I knew where all of the 1's were within the major scale shapes, this is the way that I learned the melodic minor shapes.

I DON'T recommend doing this. It is an even less standard way of doing things and its a lot easier to talk about and use the melodic minor scale if you learn it as the major scale with a flatted 3rd. STOP READING HERE AND MOVE ON TO THE NEXT PAGE...

For those of you who are curious about different ways of thinking about music theory... let me explain. The G melodic minor scale consists of the following notes:
G A Bb C D E F# G.
This is, quite obviously, the G major scale with a flatted 3rd. However, if you look at this same scale differently, you could see that it is also the F major scale with a "sharped 1".

G Melodic minor scale:     G A Bb C D E F# G
F Major scale with a # 1: F# G A Bb C D E F#

This would mean re-drawing all 7 major scale patterns with a #1. The melodic minor scale name would then be derived from the "2" of this scale. This the way that I learned the melodic minor scale... I don't recomend this. THIS IS THE ROAD LESS TRAVELED!

# WHOLE TONE

Here is the 1st scale that you'll need to know for improvising that does NOT relate to the major scale patterns (that's the bad news). BUT the good news is that it's a super easy scale to learn and use. It basically has one pattern that repeats all the way up the neck.

As the name implies, this scale is built with only whole steps. Since you've only got whole steps, the whole tone scale is going to have one less note per octave than the major scale (the major scale has a couple of half steps in it).

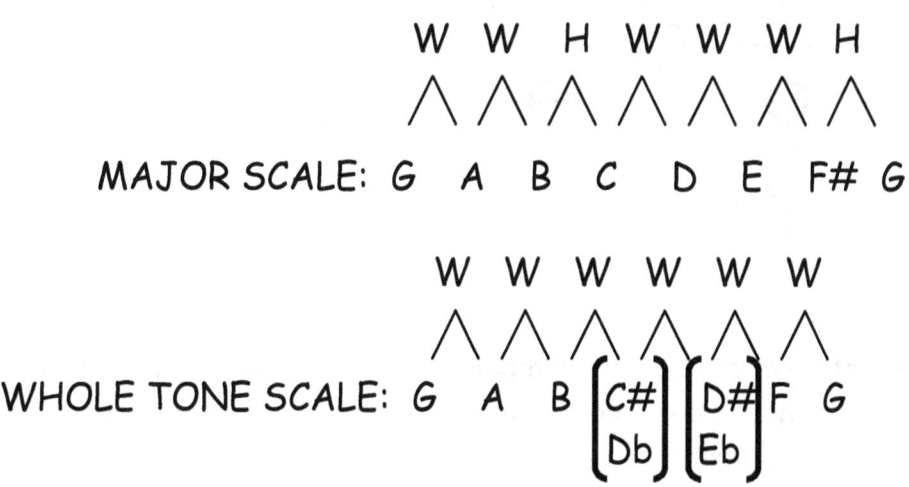

As you can see, the whole tone scale has only 6 different notes within an octave. The notes that are in the parenthesis are the two names given to that one note. So a C# is the same thing as a Db. When one note has two names, these two names are referred to as "enharmonic" (the same).

Since all of the intervals are equal in the whole tone scale (all whole steps), ALL of the notes are equally important. This means that any one of these notes could be considered the root (the name) of the scale. So this scale that appears above can be called the G, A, B, C# or Db, D# or Eb, OR the F whole tone scale. It is all of these scales wrapped up into one.

AND since this scale includes every other note on the neck of the guitar (half of the notes... 6 out of 12), then the same scale, moved up or down a half step (1 fret) will give you all of the other notes on the neck of the guitar. This means that there are only 2 whole tone scales to learn, each with 6 different names (not counting the enharmonic names as 2)... and they'll both have the same shapes!

# WHOLE TONE SCALE

Here now is the pattern for the whole tone scale. Because the whole tone scale is all whole steps, you can play this same shape every 2 frets on the guitar, and it will remain the same scale ...WAHOOOEEE!!

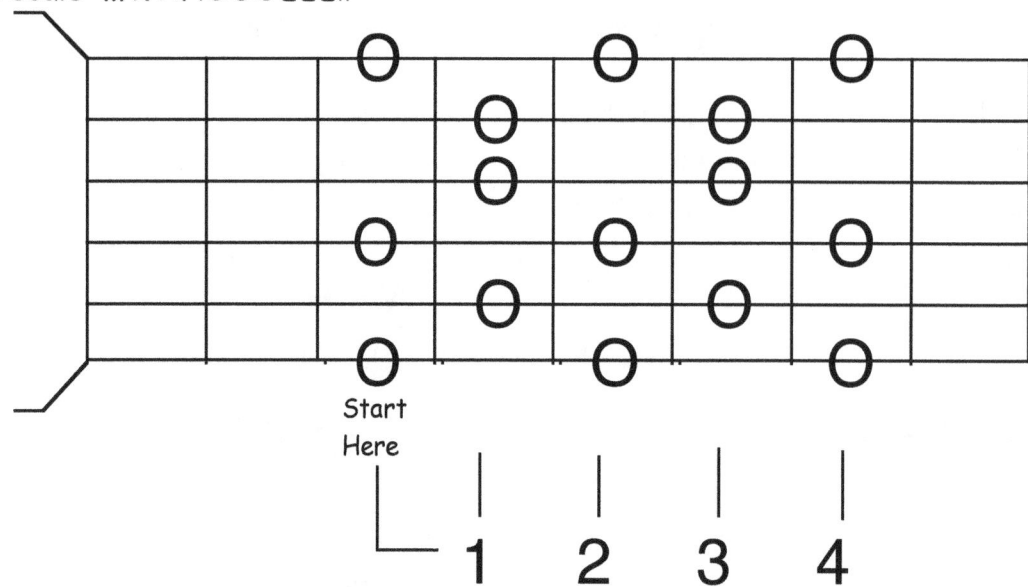

There are many, many different ways of slicing and dicing this scale up in order to play it across the neck. Once you get it under your fingers, you'll be able to ice-skate around pretty easily with this one. We've all heard this whole tone sound on TV and in movies. Its the sound they typically use when someone is "..getting very sleepy..." or if they are describing a dream sequence.

You'll really be able to hear this once I give you some of the common chords that are associated with the whole tone sound (augmented chords), but first you should see what the whole tone scale looks like on the entire neck...

Here is a diagram of the whole tone scale on the entire neck of the guitar (or at least 15 frets of it). This should help you to visualize the whole tone scale all over the neck of the guitar. Remember that you can shift the highlighted notes of this scale 2 frets in either direction and it will still be the same whole tone scale (and the same shape).

# AUGMENTED CHORDS

"Root on the low E string" Augmented chord in the whole tone pattern:

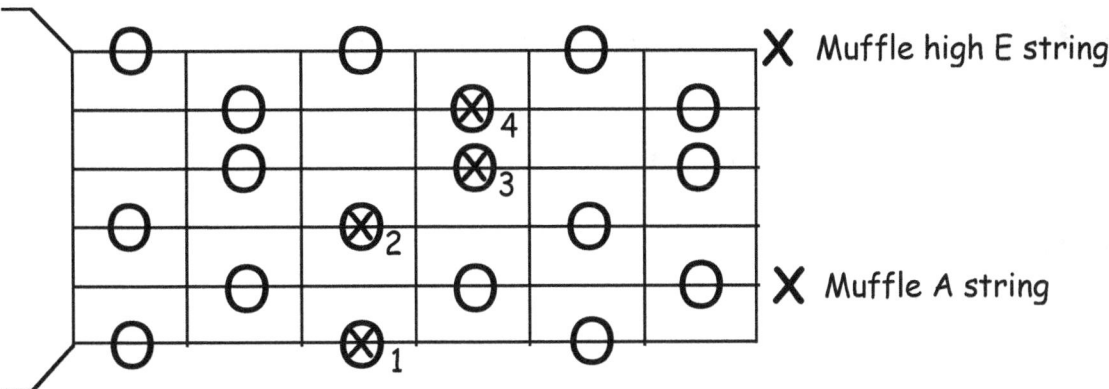

These numbers represent the left hand fingers you should use to play these notes. Since the whole tone scale repeats every 2 frets, this exact same chord voicing can be used every 2 frets, sliding up and back on the neck. While this chord can be slid around in the whole tone scale, if it is used within any other scale or sound, sliding this chord around won't work quite as well. However, your ears will have to be the judge in this matter. Here now is this augmented chord on top of the entire whole tone scale...

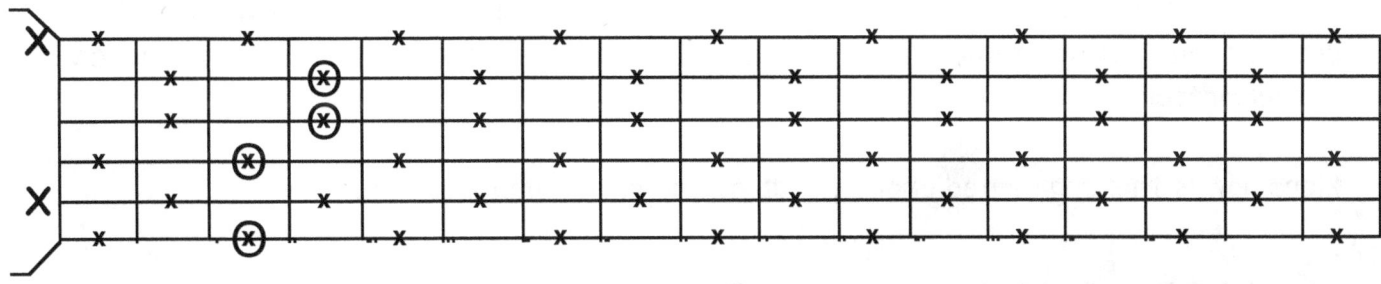

# AUGMENTED CHORDS

"Root on the A String" Augmented chord in the whole tone pattern:

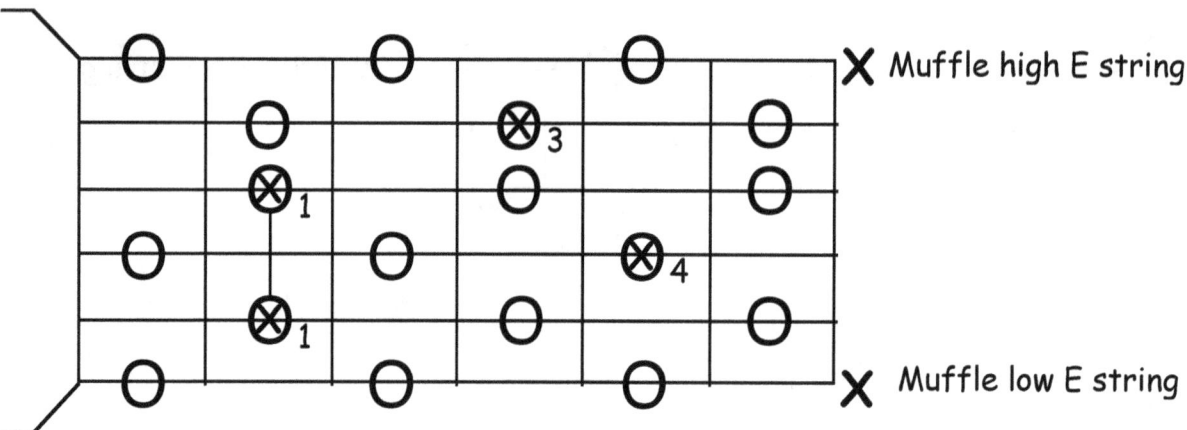

These numbers represent the left hand fingers you should use to play these notes.... AND yes, this is a type of barre chord. Your 1st finger has to barre down across the neck (make sure that you don't get the high E string to sound. This note is not in the chord... or the scale.

Again, since the whole tone scale repeats every 2 frets, this exact same chord voicing can be used every 2 frets, sliding up and back on the neck.

While this chord can be slid around in the whole tone scale, if it is used within any other scale or sound, it won't work quite as well. But again, your ears will have to be the judge in this matter.

Here now is this augmented chord on top of the entire whole tone scale...

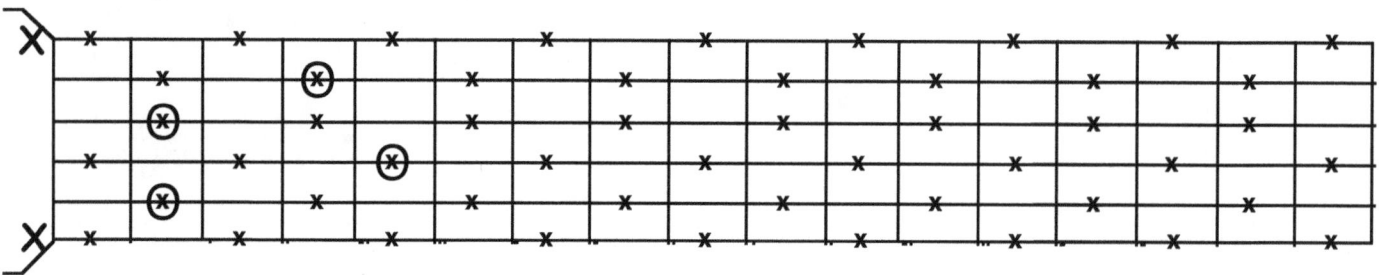

# AUGMENTED CHORDS

"Root on the D string" Augmented chord in the whole tone pattern:

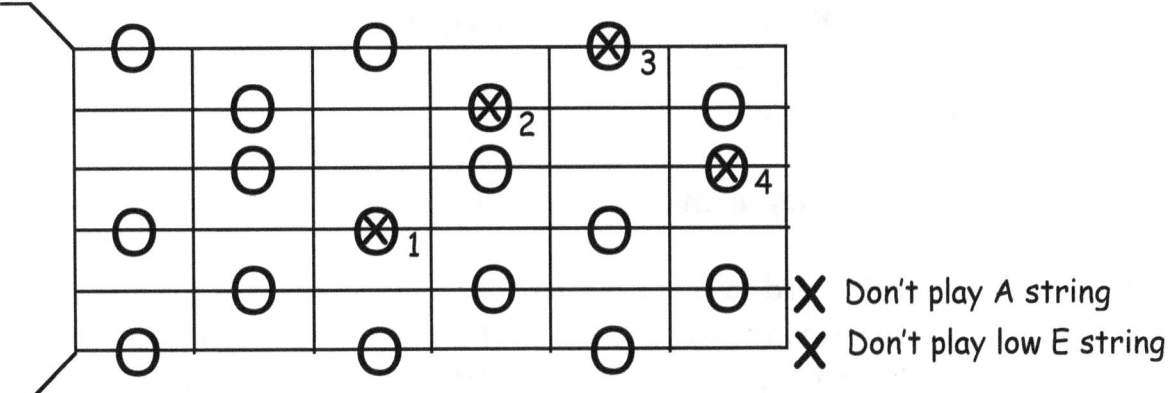

Again, these numbers represent the left hand fingers you should use to play these notes. And since the whole tone scale repeats every 2 frets, this exact same chord voicing can be used every 2 frets, sliding up and back on the neck.
Here is this augmented chord on top of the entire whole tone scale...

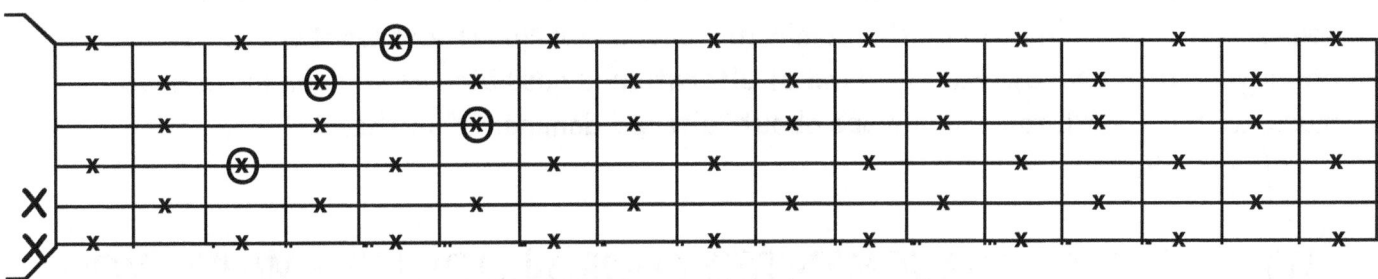

Here's another augmented chord. I've included this one because it's so easy to play. Its also super easy to slide around on the whole tone scale.

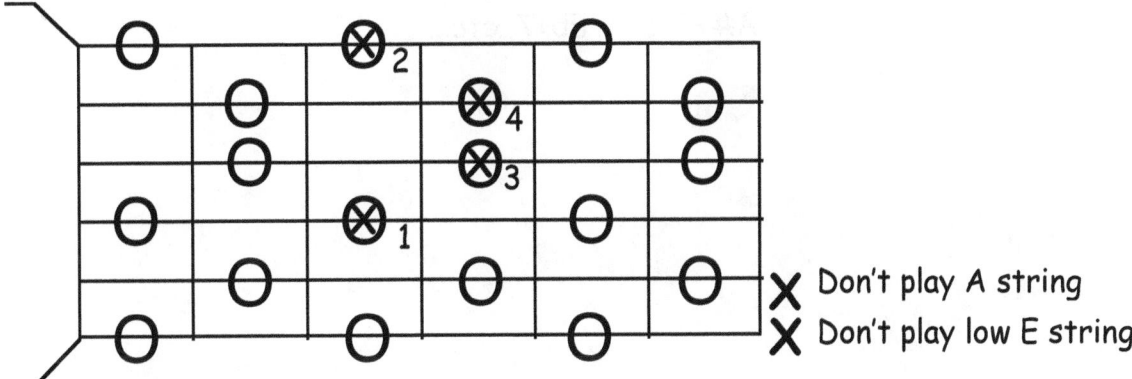

Once you've gotten the whole tone shape down, you've shifted it around on the neck, tying the identical neighboring patterns together, making sure to stay in the same whole tone scale on the entire neck (phew yet again), you should then transpose the whole thing into the other key(s). This just means sliding everything up or down 1 fret and begin soloing again.

## HOW DO YOU USE THIS SCALE?

There are many uses for the whole tone scale.

For now, I'll give you at least one way in which you can use this scale:

When you're given a dominant7 chord to solo over (a chord built on the 5th scale degree of a major scale), instead of playing the major scale that the 5 chord comes from, you can play the whole tone scale that starts with the same letter name of the dominant7 chord.

So if you are given a D dominant7 chord to solo over, rather than playing in the key of G major, you could also solo in D whole tone.

This scale doesn't "exactly" fit all of the notes of the dominant7 chord. It provides a sound that sharps the 5th of the dominant7 chord (turning it into what we've been calling an "augmented" chord). But this kind of alteration is possible... if you can make good music with it. We'll talk much more about "altered dominants" in the...
...Major Method Vol. 2.

## WHAT DOES AN AUGMENTED CHORD LOOK LIKE WHEN YOU READ A CHORD CHART?

Usually an augmented chord looks like a dominant7 chord with a "plus sign" in between the letter name and the 7:

D+7, A#+7, C+7, Eb+7, etc....

# DIMINISHED

Here is the 2nd scale that you'll have to know that does NOT relate to the major scale patterns..... bummer. But there is some good news!

The diminished scale has a symmetrical intervalic structure..... (WHAT?!?!). All of the intervals of the diminished scale follow a pattern. This pattern repeats itself every 3 frets. This means that we are basically going to have only one pattern to learn on the neck.

The intervalic pattern for the diminished scale is an alternating pattern:
whole step, half step, whole step, half step, etc...

So this is pretty different from either the major patterns or the whole tone pattern(s):

```
                      W  W  H  W  W  W  H
                      ∧  ∧  ∧  ∧  ∧  ∧  ∧
       MAJOR SCALE:   G  A  B  C  D  E  F# G


                         W   W    W    W   W  W
                         ∧   ∧    ∧    ∧   ∧  ∧
    WHOLE TONE SCALE:  G  A  B  [C#] [D#] F  G
                                [Db] [Eb]


                      W  H   W   H   W  H   W   H
                      ∧  ∧   ∧   ∧   ∧  ∧   ∧   ∧
    DIMINISHED SCALE: G  A [A#]  C [C#][D#] E [F#] G
                           [Bb]    [Db][Eb]   [Gb]
```

All right, let's get a look at what these intervals look like on the neck of the guitar...

# DIMINISHED SCALE

Here is one way of playing the diminished scale on the neck of the guitar. Use one finger per fret for this pattern (starting with your 1st finger on the 3rd fret). This pattern will require that you shift your left hand to the left, one fret, once you get to the D string (You do remember which string is the D string don't you?).

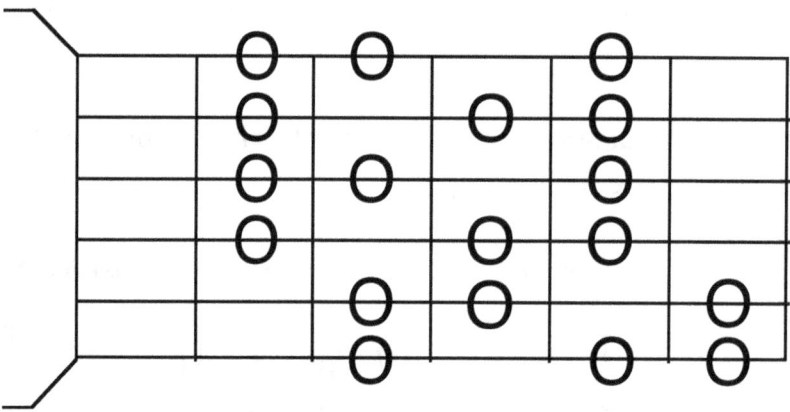

So, basically, your left hand fingers are playing: 1, 3, 4... 1, 2, 4... 1, 3, 4... 1, 2, 4, etc... Here is the diminished scale on the entire neck of the guitar. I've drawn lines to outline the diminished pattern. You can see how the pattern just repeats itself as you travel up the neck. Once you are in the pattern, it's pretty easy and life is good. Trouble begins when you start shifting from one pattern to the next and you are in between the patterns. It will take some practice and concentration to shift between patterns and not get lost!

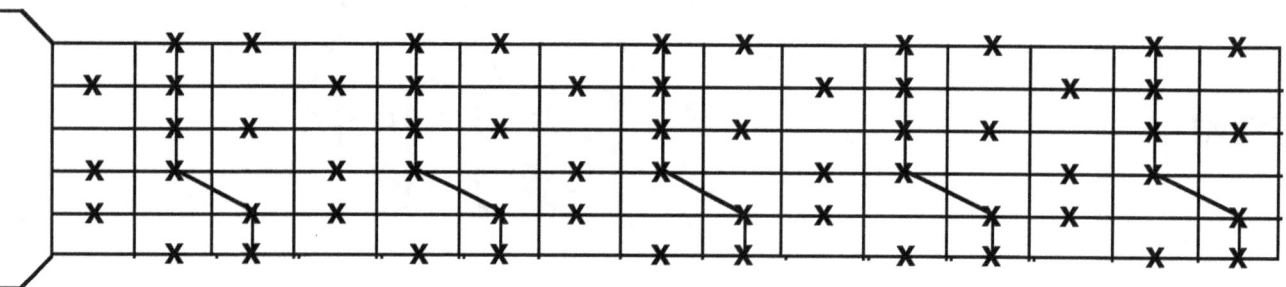

# DIMINISHED CHORDS

*"Root on the E low string" Diminished chord in the diminished pattern:

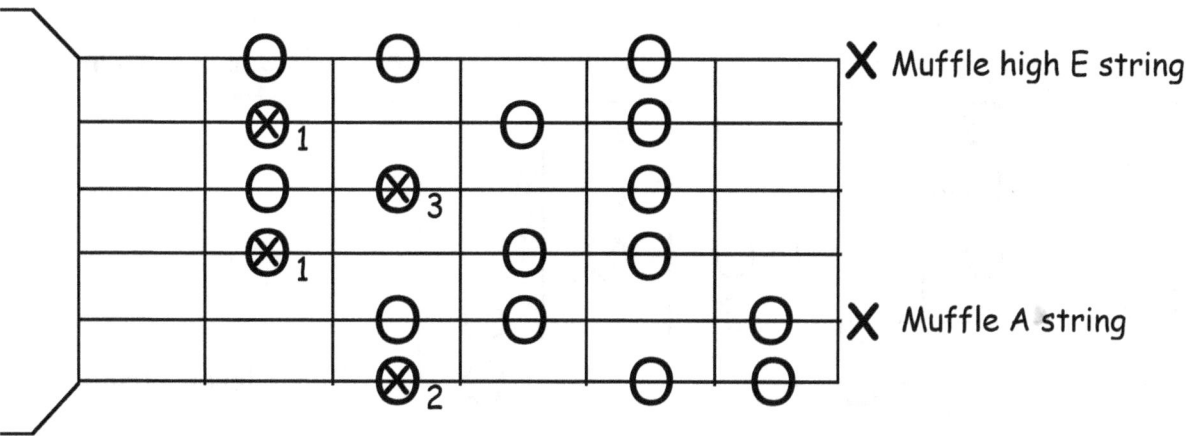

\* This label is a bit misleading. The notes of the diminished chord are structured so that any of the notes of this chord can be considered the root of the chord.

These numbers represent the left hand fingers you should use to play these notes.

Since the diminished scale repeats every 3 frets, this exact same chord voicing can be used every 3 frets, sliding up and back on the neck (not counting the fret that you're on).

AND yes again, this is a type of partial barre chord. Your 1st finger has to barre down across the neck (make sure that you don't get the high E string to sound. This note is not in the chord).

Here now is this diminished chord on top of the entire diminished scale...

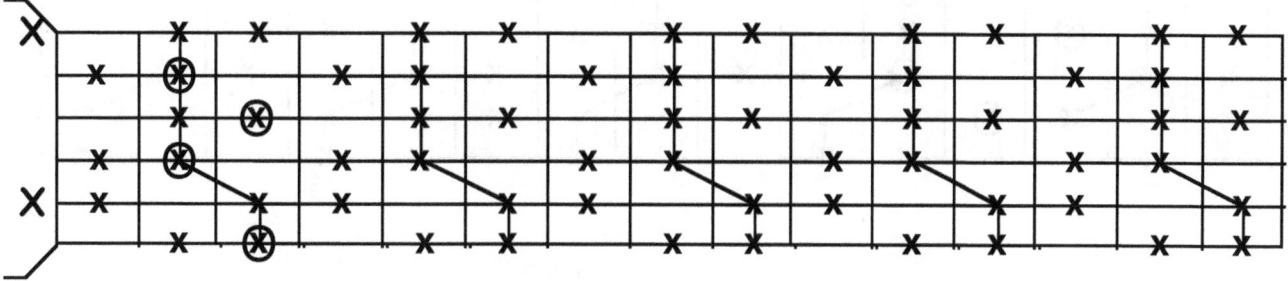

# DIMINISHED CHORDS

*"Root on the A string" Diminished chord in the diminished pattern:

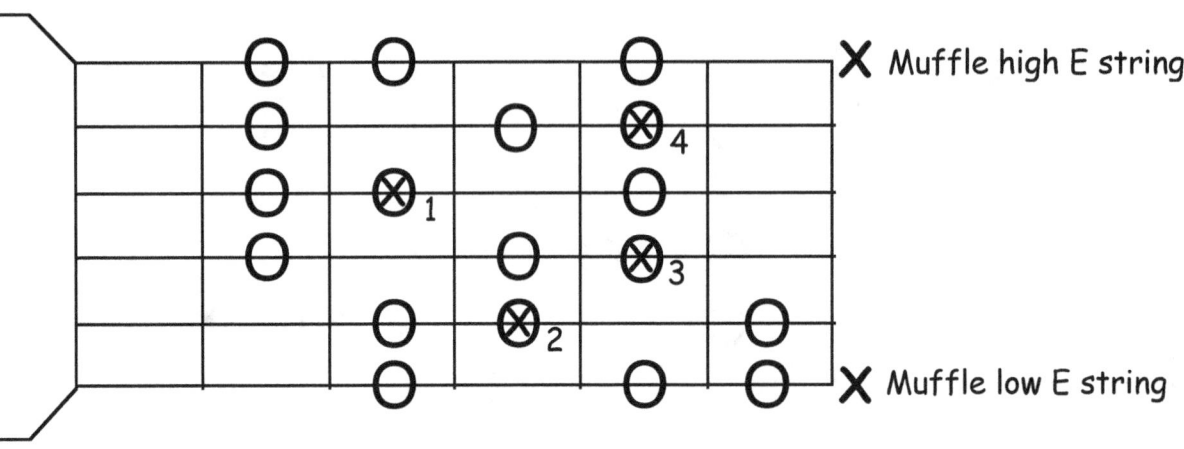

* This label is a bit misleading. The notes of the diminished chord are structured so that any of the notes of this chord can be considered the root of the chord.

These numbers represent the left hand fingers you should use to play these notes.

Again, since the diminished scale repeats every 3 frets, this exact same chord voicing can be used every 3 frets, sliding up and back on the neck (not counting the fret that you're on).

Here now is this diminished chord on top of the entire diminished scale...

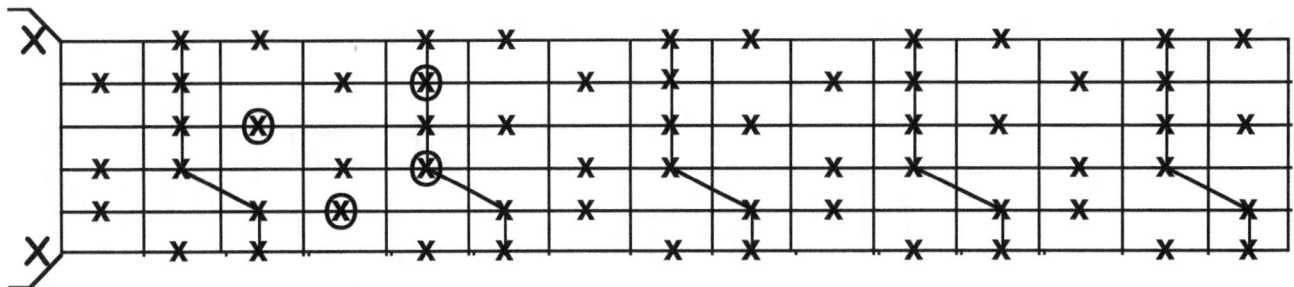

# DIMINISHED CHORDS

*"Root on the D string" Diminished chord in the diminished pattern:

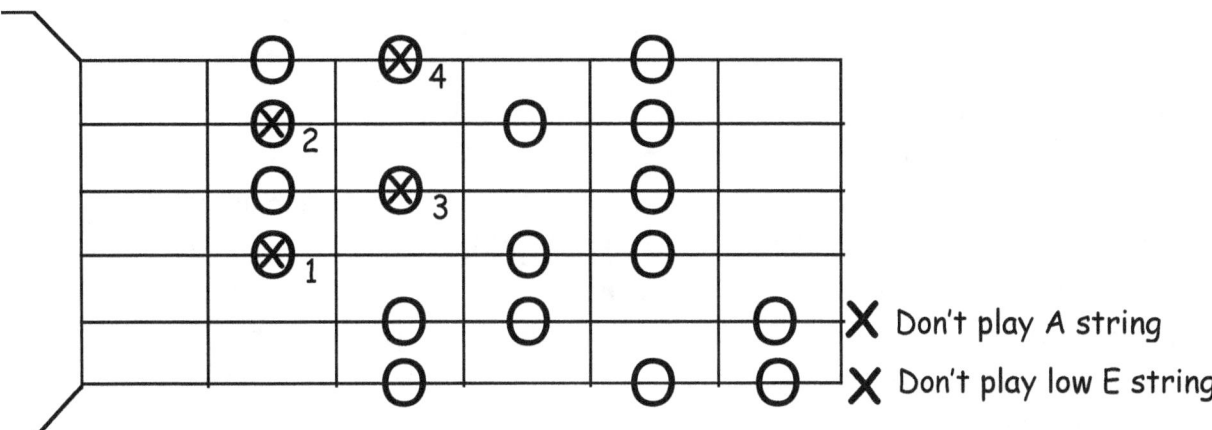

X Don't play A string
X Don't play low E string

\* This label is a bit misleading. The notes of the diminished chord are structured so that any of the notes of this chord can be considered the root of the chord.

These numbers represent the left hand fingers you should use to play these notes.

Again, since the diminished scale repeats every 3 frets, this exact same chord voicing can be used every 3 frets, sliding up and back on the neck (not counting the fret that you're on).

Here now is this diminished chord on top of the entire diminished scale...

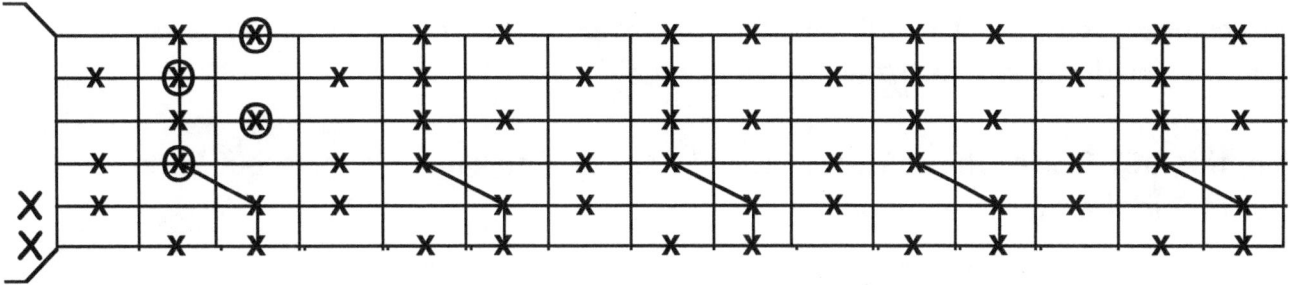

Once you've gotten the diminished shape down, you've shifted it around on the neck (every 3 frets), tying the identical neighboring patterns together, making sure to stay in the same diminished scale on the entire neck (this shifting business will be a little more difficult than with the whole tone scale), you should then transpose the whole thing into the other two possible diminished keys. This just means sliding everything up 1 fret (for one of the keys), and up 2 frets (for the other possible diminished key) and begin soloing again.

Remember that the diminished scale repeats itself every 3 frets. So there are only 3 different diminished keys possible. You can only play 2 NEW diminished scales before you're back in the original key... 3 frets up or down. Of course, in music, we still use all 12 possible letter names to refer to these three keys (ugh!!). You've just got to remember which ones are the same. Here are the various names that you may encounter for the 3 different diminished scales. The names with the "/" between them are the same note with two different names (enharmonic names for one note.... if this doesn't sound familiar, you should review the "chromatic scale" section in the early part of this book):

1) G, A#/Bb, C#/Db, E
2) G#/Ab, B, D, F
3) A, C, D#/Eb, F#/Gb

## HOW DO YOU USE THIS SCALE?

There are many uses for the diminished scale. For now, I'll give you at least one way in which you can use this scale:

When you're given a dominant7 chord to solo over (a 5 chord), instead of playing the major scale that the 5 chord comes from, you can play the diminished scale that starts one fret above the letter name of the dominant7 chord.

So if you are given a D dominant7 chord to solo over, rather than playing in the key of G major, you could also solo in D# or Eb diminished.

Again, this DOES alter the dominant7 chord. And we'll talk much more about "altered dominants" in the... Major Method Vol. 2.

## WHAT DOES A DIMINISHED CHORD LOOK LIKE WHEN YOU READ A CHORD CHART?

Usually a diminished chord looks like a dominant7 chord with a small "o" sign in between the letter name and the 7:   Do7, A#o7, Co7, Ebo7, etc....

# CYCLE OF WHAT?!?

Just when you thought that you have been given way too much information... here's a way to organize some of it!

When you're trying to write a song or figure out someone else's song, and you don't know what chords to use or where to begin, there are some patterns that are common in music that can help you. Most music works well because the chords of the song "go" well with each other.

Knowing what each chord's tendencies are will help you in organizing your sounds. I'll now give you a bunch of general guidelines (...and I mean general... I'm a firm believer in bending, twisting, and breaking rules... as long as it sounds GOOD!!)

In any major key you have 7 possible chords. Here are the basic functions of these 7 chords:

- The 1, 6, and 3 chords are basically "stable" chords (and in this order... the 1 is the most stable, the 6 is the next most stable, and the 3 is the next most stable). Stable means that these chords are good chords to start with or end with. They seem to have a stability that makes our ear comfortable hearing them as a starting place or a resting place....
  ...your ears may differ... AND THIS IS OK!!

- The 2 and 4 chords are thought of as set up chords. These are chords that prepare the ear for something new.

- The 5 and the 7 chords are thought of as TENSION chords. These are chords that the ear tends to want to RELEASE to a more stable chord (like a 1, 6, or 3 chord).

Music is frequently all about this harmonic TENSION and RELEASE. So you may start out "stable", move to less stability, "set up" for tension, arrive at "tension", and finally release back to "stable".

A common example of this kind of motion through music is the following chord progression:

**1** (stable), **6** (a little less stable), **2** (moving to set up tension), **5** (full of tension and wanting to be resolved), **1** (Ahhh! Finally back to stability)

If you were in the key of G major and you gave each chord of this progression one measure, the chord progression would look like this:

## 1, 6, 2, 5, 1 CHORD PROGRESSION

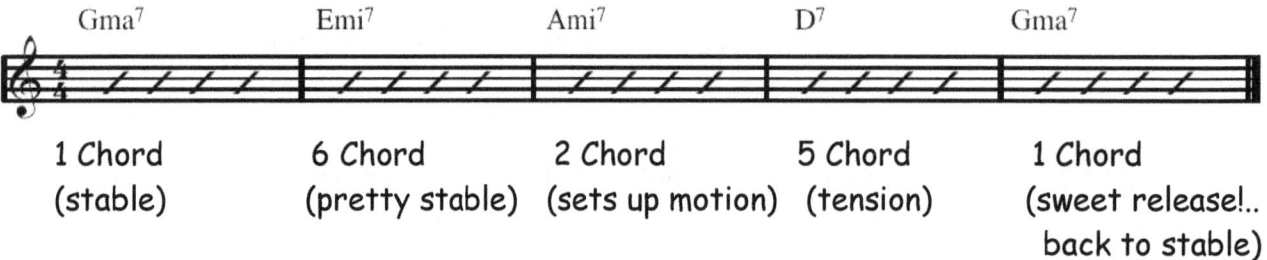

| 1 Chord | 6 Chord | 2 Chord | 5 Chord | 1 Chord |
| (stable) | (pretty stable) | (sets up motion) | (tension) | (sweet release!.. back to stable) |

So you've got these chord motion tendencies to help organize sound when you're in one key. There are also common "root motions" that our ears tend to gravitate towards. The two strongest (and, yes this could be disputed) root motions are:

1) Half Steps.... F# to G or Ab to G....... C# to D or Eb to D .... etc...

2) 5 to 1 root motion...  Let me explain.

Do you recall your major scale intervalic structure? ....Remember that the letter name of the key that you're in is called the 1... so in the key of G major, G is the 1.
And in G major, D is the 5th scale degree. So D is the 5 of G in the key
of G major.

```
                        1   2   3   4   5   6   7   1
           MAJOR SCALE: G   A   B   C   D   E   F#  G
```

103

The 5-1 root movement, in this case between the D (5) and the G (1), is considered to be one of the strongest chord movements in music. Some classical music ends with a repetition of the 5 chord resolving to the 1 chord over and over:
5-1, 5-1, 5-1.........5......1. This helps to finally establish the tonality of the piece in the audiences' ear and it provides for a strong and definitive ending.

Today this root motion is used in many chord progressions. One way to learn all of the possible 5-1 progressions is through what is called....

# ..."THE CYCLE OF 5THS"

This cycle can be drawn as a wheel with all of the 5-1 relationships that are possible in our 12 tone system of music. If you start at the top with the key of C major (no sharps or flats) you then move to the right to the key of F major (C is the 5 in the key of F). After this comes the key of Bb (F is the 5 in the key of Bb), then the key of Eb (Bb is the 5 in the key of Eb), and so on.

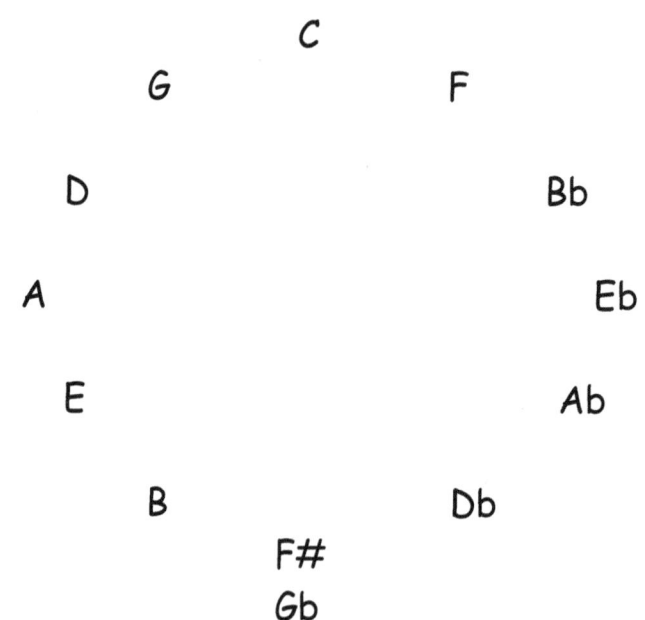

NOTE: This "**Cycle** Of 5th's" that is used in improvisational music, is the exact mirror of the "**Circle** Of 5th's" that is taught in classical music. More traditionl music theorists would call this "Cycle of 5ths" the "Circle of 4ths".

Remember that the F# and the Gb are the same note with two names... ...and when one note has two names, these two names are referred to as... ..."enharmonic" (Did you remember this or did I have to tell you?).

We could talk a lot more about this cycle of 5th's, but the most important thing that you can do right now is to *memorize* it....(I know that this is a tough word for most of us, but ...DO IT!!).

Many, many, many.... (did I say many?) chord progressions us this cycle AT LEAST in part. Knowing the **CYCLE OF 5THS** will make learning new tunes happen A LOT faster. You will be able to see these letter name relationships in the chord progression of a song, recognize them as 5-1 relationships and be able to understand the harmonic motion of the composition much more quickly (this means that you'll be able to play a new tune like you've known it you're whole life, and you won't be worrying about how all of the chords relate to each other).

In fact, let's look back at the chord progression that we used as an example of a common progression (1, 6, 2, 5, 1). Once you figure out what the letter names of each of these notes are (in G major they're: G, E, A, D, G), you'll notice that all of the root movements from the E on, are ALL 5-1 root relationships. The E to the A (5-1), the A to the D (5-1) and the D to the G ....they're ALL 5-1 root relationships. This is a perfect example of a chord progression that is going through "the cycle" within one key. This is another reason why this chord progression sounds "good".

Another way of figuring out this 5-1 business is to calculate by numbers. If you're on a 6 chord and you count down 5 numbers, including the one that you start with, you can figure out the 5-1 relationship. So if you're on a 6 chord, you'd count: **6, 5, 4, 3, 2**. Here the 6 chord is the "5" of the 2 chord because the 2 chord is 5 chords down from the 6 chord.

So the 5-1 thing can happen "diatonically" (within one key). But it can also be used "nondiatonically". Using this 5-1 movement in a nondiatonic manor is a common way for a composer/improviser to:

1) Slightly vary the given material in order to spice things up a bit.

2) Get out of the key that they're in and move into a completely different key.

Let's deal with the 1st of these uses for the non diatonic 5-1 root motion. The following is an example of how these different uses of the 5-1 movement can spice up an otherwise diatonic chord progression.

NOTE: In improvisational theory the term "diatonic" is used to refer to notes or chords that are in the same key (derived from the same scale). In classical theory or common practice period theory, the term "diatonic" has a slightly different definition and usage.

GIVEN THESE CHORDS:

## 1, 6, 2, 5, 1 DIATONIC CHORD PROGRESSION

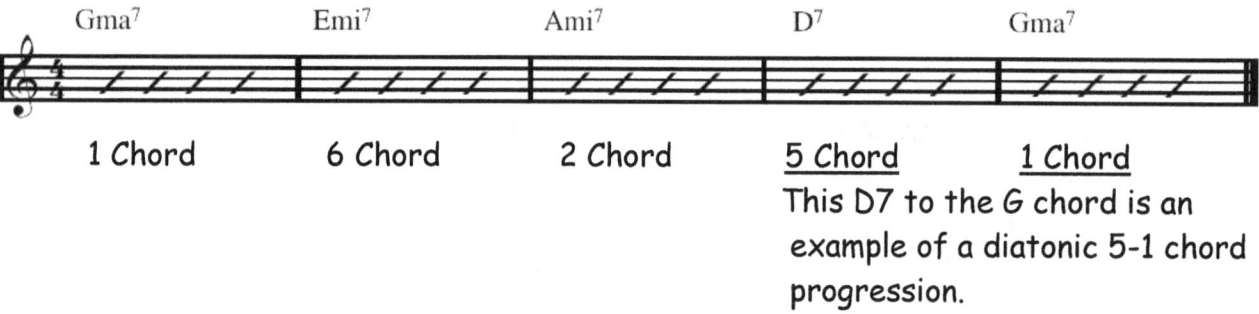

1 Chord     6 Chord     2 Chord     5 Chord     1 Chord

This D7 to the G chord is an example of a diatonic 5-1 chord progression.

## 1, "6", "2", 5, 1 NONDIATONIC CHORD PROGRESSION

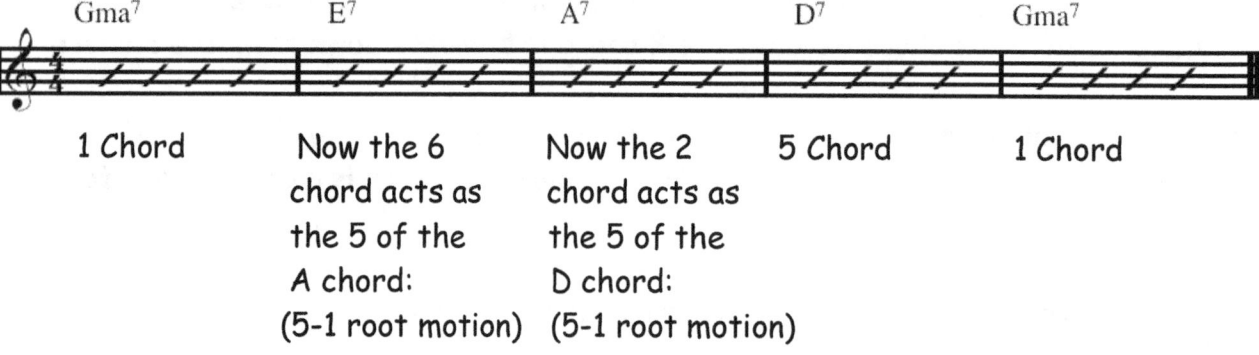

1 Chord     Now the 6 chord acts as the 5 of the A chord: (5-1 root motion)     Now the 2 chord acts as the 5 of the D chord: (5-1 root motion)     5 Chord     1 Chord

This chord progression is referred to as nondiatonic because the E7 chord is the 5 chord in the key of A major. And the A7 chord is the 5 chord in the key of D major. Neither of these chords are diatonic to the key of G major (which is the key that we started in).

This also means that when you are soloing or trying to write a melody over these two chords, you have to use the notes from the A major scale for the E7 chord and the D major scale for the A7 chord.

## The 4th to the 5th measures:

If you look at the D7 to the G major7, you can see that the G major7 chord is the "target" chord for the D7 chord. This G major7 is the chord that releases the harmonic tension that the D7 chord has created. This D7 is considered to be the 5 of the 1 chord (Gmajor7) and it keeps you in the key of G major.

## The 3rd to the 4th measures:

Since the A minor7 chord has been changed to an A dominant7 chord, it now functions as the 5 of the D chord (A is 5 of D). So for the duration of the A7 chord, you are temporarily in the key of D major.

Also, since the D chord is the 5 chord in the key of G major, the A7 is considered to be the 5 of the 5 chord (yes, too many name and number references).

## The 2nd to the 3rd measures:

Since the E minor7 chord has been changed to an E dominant7 chord, it now functions as a 5 of the A chord. So for the duration of the E7 chord, you are temporarily in the key of A major.

And now since the A chord has been changed to a 5 of the D chord (the 5 of the 5), the E7 is considered to be the 5 of the 5, of the 5! YES, this is a little ridiculous, but it IS a really cool way of turning a diatonic chord progression into a juicy, harmonically rich chord progression.

Because this "reharmonization" of the chords travels backwards through the cycle of 5ths, it is called "BACK-CYCLING".

All right, lets deal with the use of nondiatonic 5-1 chords in order to completely change the key that you are in. The 5 chord (dominant7 chord) is so full of tension that it can act as a harmonic worm-hole that allows you to slip into another key without much notice.

You can arbitrarily (although one would hope that you've put some thought and ears into the matter) replace any chord with a dominant7 chord and use it to take you into another key. If you follow this newly added dominant7 chord with it's new target 1 chord, the harmonic motion is strong enough to establish this new key as home.

Let's now take a look at how you can use one of these "non-diatonic" 5-1 worm holes and see how it works...

Here is an example of how the use of the 5-1 movement can get you completely out of the key that you're in and move you into another key.

GIVEN THESE CHORDS: ...again!

## 1, 6, 2, 5, 1 DIATONIC CHORD PROGRESSION

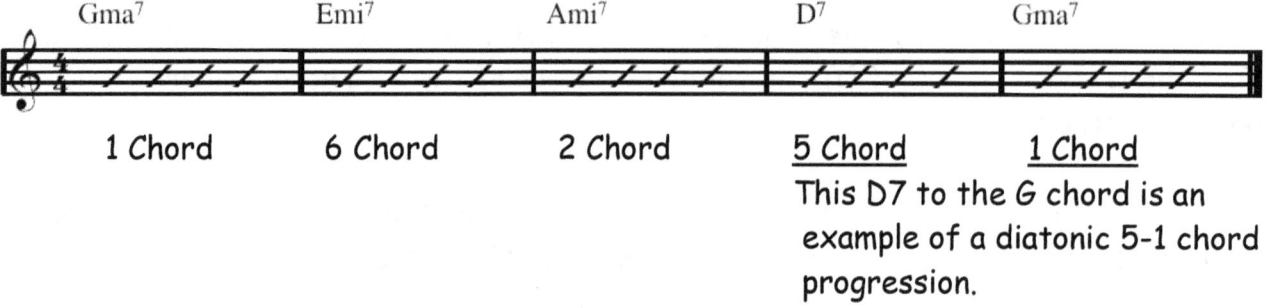

1 Chord     6 Chord     2 Chord     5 Chord     1 Chord

This D7 to the G chord is an example of a diatonic 5-1 chord progression.

YOU COULD CHANGE THINGS UP LIKE THIS:

## USING THE 5-1 CHORD PROGESSION TO CHANGE KEYS

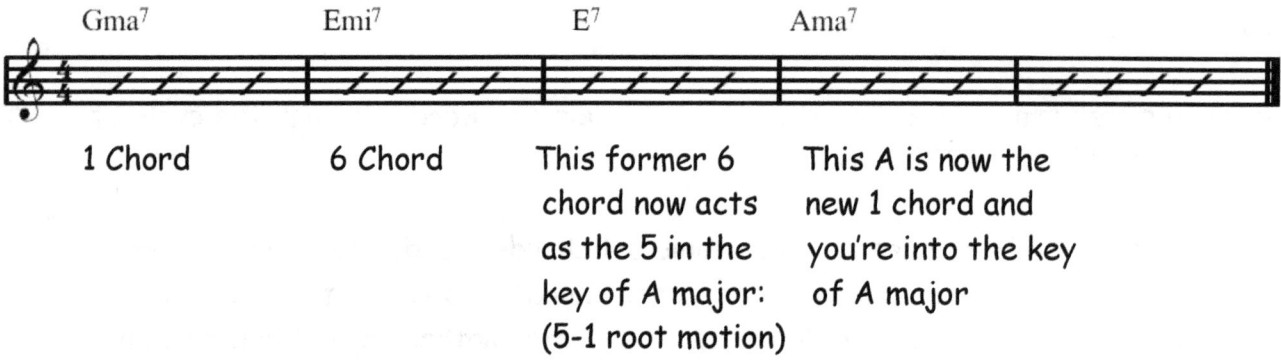

1 Chord     6 Chord     This former 6 chord now acts as the 5 in the key of A major: (5-1 root motion)     This A is now the new 1 chord and you're into the key of A major

In this example of "USING THE 5-1 CHORD PROGRESSION TO CHANGE KEYS", the 1st two measures remain as the unassuming 1 chord and 6 chord in the key of G major. The A minor7 (from the 3rd measure of the old diatonic example) has been changed to an E dominant7th chord (5 chord in the key of A major). Then, instead of going to the old diatonic D dominant7th chord in the 4th measure (which would have brought us back to the key of G major), it resolves to a big ol' A major7 chord, firmly establishing the new tonal center of A major.

So, for this example, the first 2 measures would be in the key of G major and the rest of the line would be in A major.

Remember, however, that many chords can function in more than one key. The opening G major7 chord can be a 1 chord in the key of G major, OR it also can be a 4 chord in the key of D major. If this was the way you decided to interpret this chord, the first 2 measures *could* be a 4-2 chord progression in the key of D major: the G major7 can be the 4 chord in D major and the E minor7 can be the 2 chord in D major (you could figure this out pretty quickly if you knew the cycle of 5ths very well AND if you learned the information provided in the chapter on four note chords).

The 5-1 progression (the E7 to the A major7), however, doesn't leave an awful lot of room for reinterpretation. Its pretty definitely in the key of A major!

But you see how any one chord progression can be interpreted in various ways. And how any one chord progression can be changed in many ways to create a completely different sounding tune.

If you want to change a chord progression, or write a new chord progression, then, using 5-1 relationships and the cycle of 5ths is a very strong way to ensure a good sounding progression.

The tension in these 5 chords (dominant 7th chords) is so strong that sometimes an entire song will be written using only dominant 7th chords. Remember that when using four note chords, 5 chords are dominant 7th chords.

**THE BLUES** is a perfect example of how a song can be written using only dominant 7th chords.

# BLUES

Here is an example of **THE BLUES** using only dominant 7th chords:

## BASIC "G" BLUES

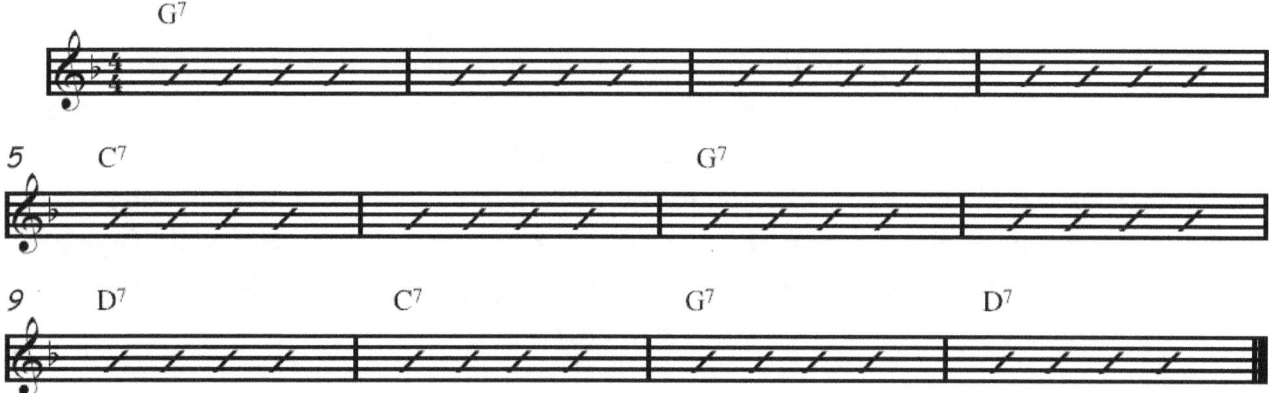

This "Blues" chord progression is called the "1,4,5 Blues". It's called this because of how all of the roots of the chords relate to each other. If G is considered to be the 1 chord, then C is its 4 chord and D is its 5 chord.

(Here's where the rules begin to bend) You know and I know that in any major scale, both the 1 chord and the 4 chord are major7 chords. BUT in the basic Blues, they are ALL played as dominant7 chords. AND for many traditional Blues players, the scale that is used over ALL 3 of these chords is the G Blues scale!

Now, you *can* play the major scales that these dominant7 chords belong to. You can also use the harmonic minor scales, the melodic minor scales, the whole tone, or the diminished scales ...BUT many people will rely heavily on the G Blues scale to solo throughout this entire chord progression.

And speaking of chord progressions, lets look at this chord progression on the neck of the guitar...

If you remember the letter names on the neck of the guitar, you'll see that the relative shape of the G, C, and D chords is this:

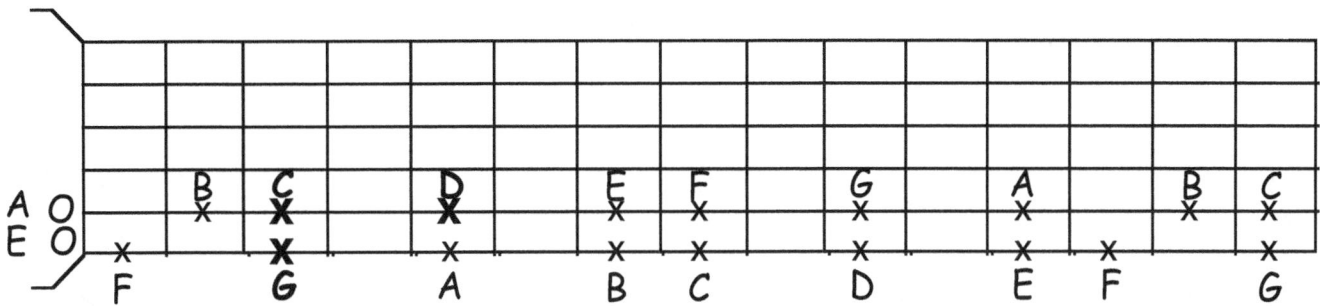

This pattern is a common pattern AND if you recall the "root relationships" within a major scale (see below), you'll notice that the G, C, and D pattern fits nicely into a 1, 4, 5 pattern.

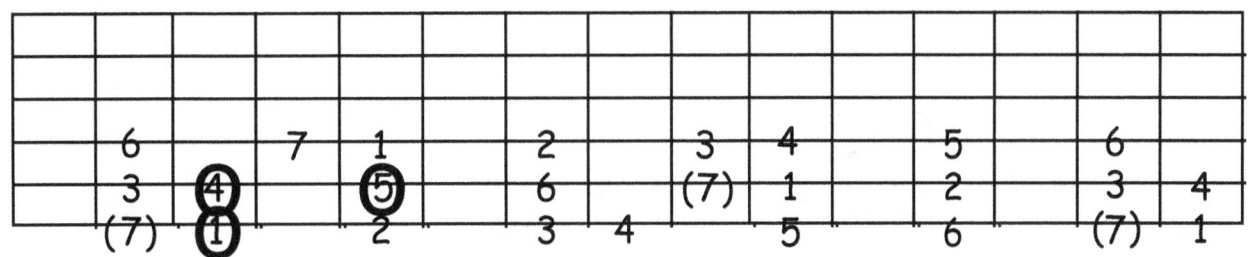

This pattern is one of the 1, 4, 5 Blues chord patterns on the neck of the guitar.

At this point, since you know three different dominant7 voicings for any one dominant7 chord (root on the low E string, root on the A string, and root on the D string), you should be able to figure out a couple other ways to play the "1, 4, 5 Blues" chord progression on the neck of the guitar.

Experiment around with the different voicings you know. See which ones you think go well together.

Also remember that the root of the 1 chord could appear on the A string or on the D string. This would mean that the relative shapes of the G, C, and D chords would look like this:

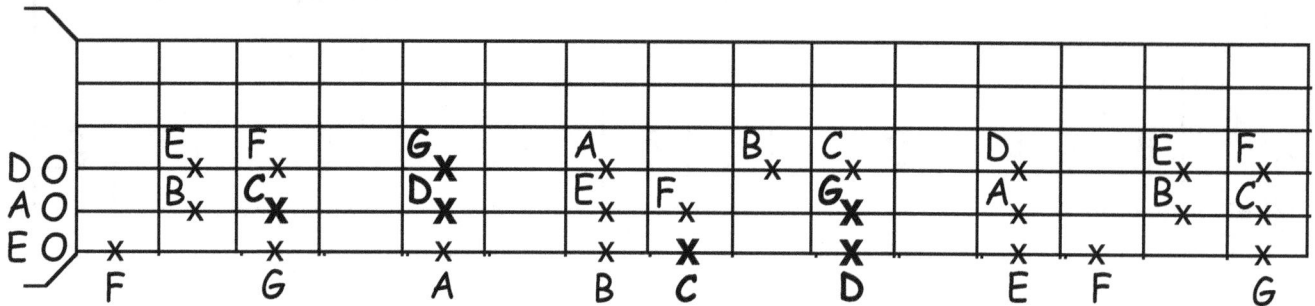

These patterns are also common patterns AND if you recall the "root relationships" within a major scale (see below), you'll notice that the G, C, and D patterns still fit nicely into the 1, 4, 5 patterns.

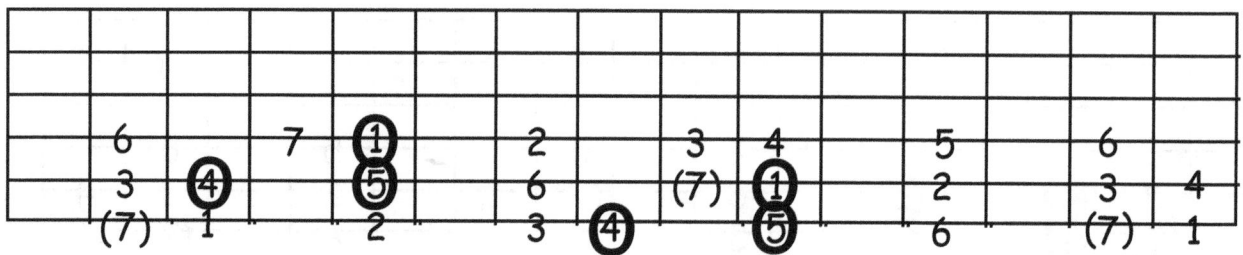

These patterns are some of the other 1, 4, 5 Blues chord patterns on the neck of the guitar. Even if you go to a different key, these patterns will work, as long as you slide them up or down in order to fit into the new key.

And again, you should be able to play these "1, 4, 5 Blues" chord progressions with those other dominant7 chord voicings that you know.

Experiment around with these different voicings. See which ones you think go well together... (does this sound familiar?)

# WHAT TO DO...

Its high time that we start using some of this information that you've learned. You now know:

I <u>SCALES</u>:
    1) Major scale (major scale & pure/natural minor scale) patterns
    2) Pentatonic scale (major & minor) patterns
    3) Blues scale patterns
    4) Harmonic minor scale patterns
    5) Melodic minor scale patterns
    6) Whole tone scale pattern(s)
    7) Diminished scale pattern(s)

II <u>CHORDS</u>:
    1) Two sets of Barre chords (three note chords)
    2) Three sets of Seventh chords (four note chords)

If someone has written a tune and they want you to play it, they will either go through the laborious task of showing you each chord and how many times they want you to play each chord over and over until you learn it... OR they will write out a chord chart and you'll be able to play it through immediately from beginning to end.

Believe me, there just isn't enough time in life to learn everything that you need to know by rote. Being able to play the chords through a chord chart and being able to solo well through a chord chart when you first see it, is a MUST. It will make you a million times more desirable in the world of music. Today this ability is considered basic. Everyone who's up for a gig will be able to play well and will play a new chart like they wrote it! Generally, you will be hired because of your musical choices, your musical personality and the voice that you've developed on your instrument (and who you know!).

You're now at the point where you need to be playing through some chord charts. You'll need to be able to access all of the chord voicings that you've learned... you did learn all of those chord voicings didn't you? And you'll need to start learning about chord/scale relations i.e. which scales go with which chords. These are the choices that will help you develop your own voice.

There are still chord inversions to learn (this will vastly increase your chord vocabulary). And then there is the great missing link between the scales and the chords: "arpeggios". This information will be included in: (drum roll please)...

# "MAJOR METHOD"
# Vol. 2

For now, I'll leave you with a chord chart that uses all of the types of 7th chords that you've learned so far. It is based on a well known "jazz standard" tune.

First, see if you can play all three seventh chord voicings that you know for each of the chords on this chart. Don't worry about playing the chart with a beat. After you are able to play all of the chord voicings that you know for each chord, try playing though the chart with a beat and only strum each chord the appropriate number of times.

Start slow! Work on your "chord-switching" and get a good sound on each of the chords.

ENJOY!!

# ALL THE CHORDS YOU KNOW

**A**

| Fmi7 | B♭mi7 | E♭7 | A♭Ma7 |

5 | D♭Ma7 | Dmi7♭5  G7 | CMa7 |

**B**

9 | Cmi7 | Fmi7 | B♭7 | E♭Ma7 |

13 | A♭Ma7 | Ami7♭5  D7 | GMa7 |

**C**

17 | Ami7 | D7 | GMa7 | |

21 | F♯mi7 | B7 | EMa7 | C+7 |

**D**

25 | Fmi7 | B♭mi7 | E♭7 | A♭Ma7 |

29 | D♭Ma7 | D♭mi7 | Cmi7 | B°7 |

33 | B♭mi7 | E♭7 | A♭Ma7 | Gmi7♭5  C7 |

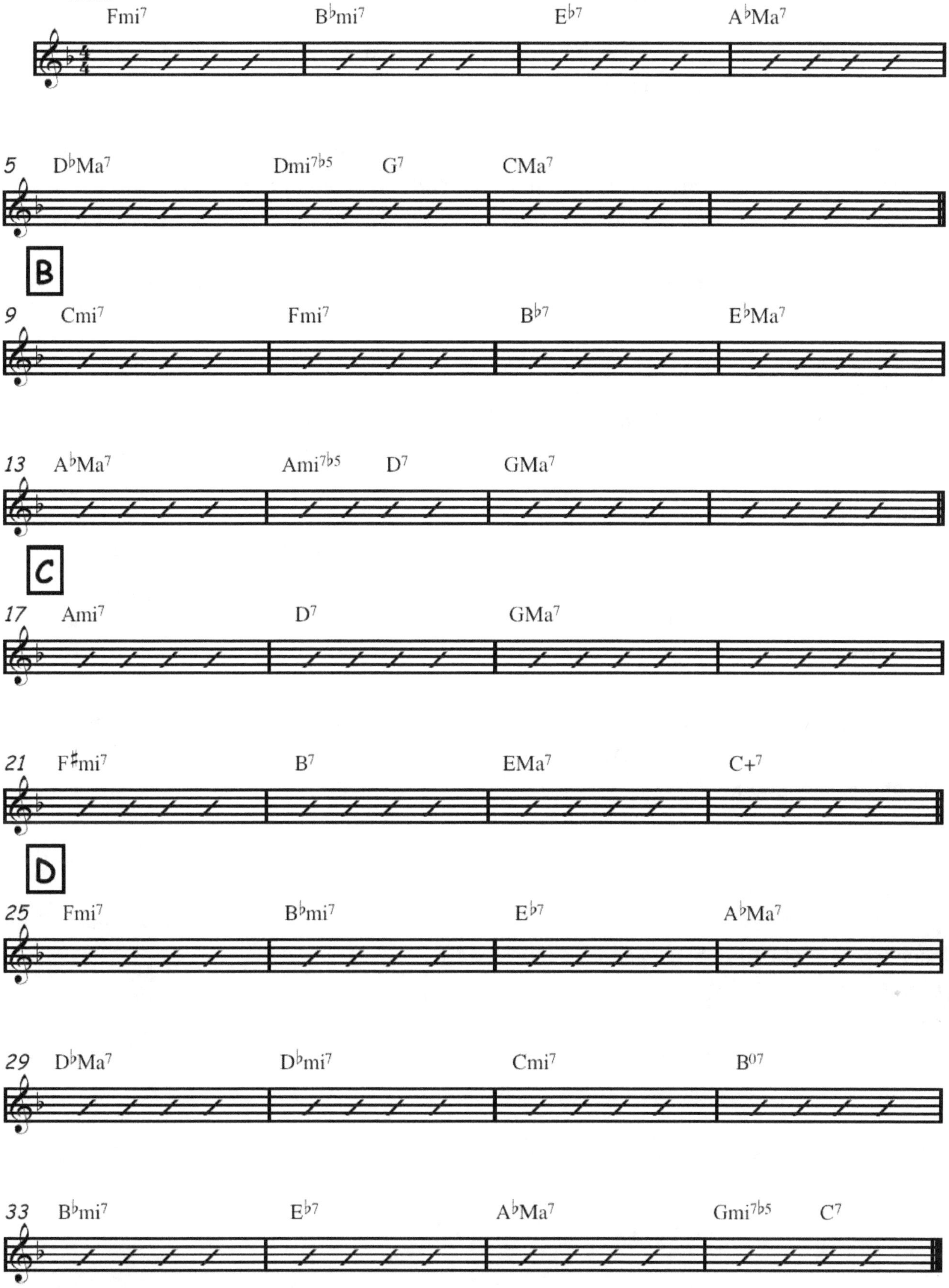

# ABOUT THE AUTHOR

**Rolf Sturm** is a NJ area guitarist who has performed and/or toured with country singer Eddy Arnold, the Tony Trischka Band, Anthony Braxton, the Argentinean tango group New York-Buenos Aires Connection, drummer Billy Martin, The Washington Street Players, Strike Anywhere Performance Ensemble, Tomas Ulrich's Cargo Cult, the Grateful Dead big band Illuminati, the Walter Thompson Orchestra, and klezmer clarinetist Giora Feidman. He has led his own NYC area bands Feed The Meter and Just Cause. He co-leads the jazz trio Tricycle, is a member of the 4 Five VI ensemble and he was the featured guitarist in *Night Music for John Lennon* under the baton of its composer, Lukas Foss.

Rolf has toured North America and Europe, performing at numerous jazz and jam band festivals, the World Expo 2000 in Hannover, Germany, at Lincoln Center and Town Hall in NYC, and at the Kennedy Center in Washington, D.C. He has performed on soundtracks for both film and television and has released numerous CDs on the Water Street Music label (www.waterstreetmusic.org), including some solo guitar CDs. Rolf has also recorded dozens of CDs as a sideman, appearing on recordings with Tony Trischka, Glen Velez, Maggie Roche, the All Terrain Band, Kloomp!, Dave Douglas, Loudon Wainright, Cameron Brown, Jorma Kaukonen, David Johansen, Ike Willis, Buddy Cage, and members of the Grateful Dead.

Rolf graduated from Ithaca College, with a BFA in Jazz Guitar, where he studied with Steve Brown. Since then he has studied with John Abercrombie, Jim Hall, Joe Pass, Bill Frisell, and Harry Leahey.

Rolf teaches jazz guitar at the Hoff-Barthelson Music School in Scarsdale, NY and in the NYC area.

To learn more about Rolf Sturm and his music visit:
www.rolfsturm.org
www.waterstreetmusic.org

www.ingramcontent.com/pod-product-compliance
Lightning Source LLC
Chambersburg PA
CBHW080517110426
42742CB00017B/3144